Guidelines for the supplementary load testing of bridges

**THE INSTITUTION OF
CIVIL ENGINEERS**

National Steering Committee for
the Load Testing of Bridges

Guidelines for the supplementary load testing of bridges

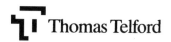 Thomas Telford

Published by Thomas Telford Publications, Thomas Telford Ltd, 1 Heron Quay, London E14 4JD
http://www.t-telford.co.uk

First published 1998

Distributors for Thomas Telford books are
USA: ASCE Press, 1801 Alexander Bell Drive, Reston, VA 20191-4400
Japan: Maruzen Co. Ltd, Book Department, 3–10 Nihonbashi 2-chome, Chuo-ku, Tokyo 103
Australia: DA Books and Journals, 648 Whitehorse Road, Mitcham 3132, Victoria

A catalogue record for this book is available from the British Library

ISBN: 0 7277 2327 0

© The Institution of Civil Engineers, 1998

Typeset by Gray Publishing, Tunbridge Wells, Kent
Printed in Great Britain by The Cromwell Press, Trowbridge, Wilts

Foreword

When the European Union implemented the 40-tonne vehicle standard in 1988 it was apparent to Highway Authorities and the Institution of Civil Engineers that the UK would be faced with a challenging programme of assessments and strengthening of the bridge stock. It was predicted that a large number of bridges would be found to have insufficient load-carrying capacity and require strengthening or replacement. At the same time it was evident that it would be inefficient to replace bridges on the evidence of calculations even if the resources could be made available. Results of assessments confirmed that a large number of bridges had inadequate load-carrying capacity but it was felt that many had reserves of strength if these could be identified. One way of showing that bridges are adequate is by load testing.

It was against this background that The National Steering Committee for Load Testing Bridges was set up as a Sub-committee of the Institution's Building and Structures Board. The task of the Committee was to produce authoritative guidance to enable practising engineers to apply load-testing techniques to existing bridges. A draft set of guidelines prepared by consultants was presented to a conference held at the Institution on 18 September 1997 and delegates were invited to comment during the discussion periods. The profession was also given the opportunity to send written comment during the following months. Many constructive and helpful communications were received and the Committee decided to appoint an external reviewer to assist the consultants to revise the guidelines in the light of the different views.

The guidelines for supplementary load testing of bridges contained in this report represent the state-of-the-art and fully meet the original objectives of the Committee. The guidelines are not prescriptive and are accompanied by background information so that there is a degree of flexibility to suit different types of bridges and situations. They provide a methodology which is not restricted to apparently understrength bridges but is also applicable to checking the performance of newly constructed bridges. Practising engineers can now benefit from authoritative guidance on the safe conduct of supplementary load testing. Most importantly, they provide a tool to aid the identification of structural actions that provide additional strengths so that apparently understrength bridges can be shown to have sufficient load-carrying capacity. It follows that this will enable highway and rail authorities to save money and resources by avoiding unnecessary strengthening and replacement. The report fills a gap in the available codes and will attract international as well as national interest

It is my pleasure to acknowledge the contributions made by members of the National Committee, their advisors, the authorities who sponsored the work, the consultants who prepared this report, the reviewer and the members of the profession who provided comment.

Sir Alan Cockshaw
President of the Institution of Civil Engineers, 1997–98

Membership of The Institution of Civil Engineers National Steering Committee For The Load Testing of Bridges

Mr David Yeoell (Chairman)	London Technical Advisors Group/LoBEG
Mr Douglas Pittam (Secretary/treasurer)	Consultant
Mr David Cliffs	London Technical Advisors Group
Mr Andrew Brodie	Scottish Office
Mr Chris Chalkley	London Borough of Enfield
Mr John Collins	Welsh Office
Dr David Cullington	Transport Research Laboratory
Dr Parag Das	Department of Environment Transport and the Regions
Mr Ronald Wilson	Institution of Civil Engineers & Department of Environment (Northern Ireland)
Mr Ashley Johnson	Mott Macdonald Group
Mr Kim Teager	Railtrack
Mr John Powell	British Waterways Board
Mr Steven Tart	Manchester Engineering Design Consultancy
Mr Peter Welch	North Yorkshire County Council/County Surveyors Society
Professor Clive Melbourne	Institution of Civil Engineers
Mr John Maguire	Lloyd's Register
Mr John Clarke	British Railways Property Board
Mr John Wilson	Institution of Civil Engineers Assistant Director of Technical Affairs

Consultants to the Committee

Dr John Menzies	Consultant
Mr Brian Pritchard	Consultant
Mr Brian Smith	Flint & Neill Partnership

The Committee would like to acknowledge the following for their contribution:

Mr Andrew Leadbeater (retired Chairman)	Oxfordshire County Council (retired)
Dr Edmund Hambly (deceased)	President ICE 1995/E Hambly Consulting
Dr Peter Lindsell	Peter Lindsell & Associates
Dr Allan Owens	Strainstall Engineering Services
Dr Shapour Mehrkar-Asl	Gifford & Partners
Mr Graham Clark	BR Research Ltd
Mr George Davidson	Institution of Structural Engineers informal study group (retired)
Mr Gordon Clemett	Technical advisors group (retired)
Mr Andrew Packham	Railtrack
Mr Richard Lavender	AMA/LoBEG Chairman (retired)

Executive summary

Bridge authorities in the UK are currently facing a large programme of bridge assessment and strengthening. This has been caused, in part, by the necessity of ensuring that the European Union deadline for allowing 40-tonne lorries on to UK roads can be met. Many bridges have failed theoretical assessments and some bridge owners, frustrated by the fact that many failed structures are apparently in good condition and showing no signs of distress, have resorted to load testing their bridges to try to provide additional information.

A National Steering Committee for the Load Testing of Bridges was set up to examine the role of bridge load testing as a tool for assisting the assessment process. The National Steering Committee consists of representatives from all major bridge owners including the Highways Agency, the County Surveyors Society, the London Bridges Engineering Group, Railtrack and the British Waterways Board. It also includes representatives from consulting engineers and universities and has the support of the Institution of Civil Engineers.

The overall objective of the National Steering Committee was to produce authoritative guidance on load-testing techniques; which could be used by the practising engineer to determine capacities of existing bridges/structures that are safe, prudent and minimize levels of restriction to the transport infrastructure.

In June 1995 the committee appointed Rendel Palmer & Tritton in association with Peter Lindsell & Associates and supported by Professors Bakht, Clark and Harding as consultants to carry out a preliminary study of all the available information on bridge load testing. They were to recommend a detailed methodology which would form the basis of a brief to consultants appointed to produce authoritative guidelines for the load testing of bridges. Their report concluded that there is a place for load testing in the evaluation of bridges and other structures and that load testing is a valid tool for bridge managers. They also concluded that there was enough information and experience available to permit safe and effective guidelines to be written. As a result of the preliminary study the National Steering Committee decided to divide the second stage work and restrict the scope of this document to guidelines for supplementary load testing. Work on proof and proving load testing is being carried out by others under the auspices of the Highways Agency.

The guidelines contained in this document were not drafted in a prescriptive form, but seek to provide advice on the appropriate use of supplementary load testing as an aid to assessment by calculation. The guidelines have been written to enable engineers to determine:

- when it is appropriate to consider the use of supplementary load testing
- the level of risk, both public safety and economic, associated with load testing
- how to plan and carry out a load test including the level of expertise necessary, the appropriate loading methods and the type and quantity of instrumentation required.

In addition, the document is intended to be a source of information on load testing, measuring equipment and specialist techniques that engineers can use for reference.

Contents

1 Introduction — 1

1.1 Background — 1
1.2 Forms of static load testing — 1
1.3 Scope of guidelines — 2
1.4 Use of guidelines — 6

2 The assessment process — 8

2.1 Objectives and procedures — 8
2.2 Inspection — 8
2.3 Materials — 9
2.4 Loading — 10
2.5 Analysis of the structure — 10
2.6 Masonry and concrete arches — 11
2.7 Strength of members — 13
2.8 Treatment of structures that do not meet the requirements of the assessment codes — 13
2.9 Summary — 14

3 Use of supplementary load testing — 15

3.1 Introduction — 15
3.2 Condition of structure — 16
3.3 Structural actions — 16
3.4 Feasibility study — 20

4 Planning the test — 22

4.1 Site visit — 22
4.2 Traffic management — 22
4.3 Loading — 22
4.4 Instrumentation — 23
4.5 Safety — 23
4.6 Risk analysis — 24
4.7 Technical approval — 24

5 Methods of load application — 26

5.1 Introduction — 26
5.2 Review of methods — 26
5.3 Railway loading — 29

6 Measuring equipment **31**

6.1 Introduction 31
6.2 Displacements 31
6.3 Strains 32
6.4 Temperature 33
6.5 Data recording 34

7 Test procedures **36**

7.1 Introduction 36
7.2 Initial planning 36
7.3 Site preparation 38
7.4 Installation of instruments 38
7.5 Load application 39
7.6 Measuring responses 40
7.7 Emergency procedures. 40
7.8 Clearance of site 40

8 Interpretation of results **42**

8.1 Introduction 42
8.2 Comparison of measured and calculated results 42
8.3 Calibration of structural models 43
8.4 Estimation of load capacity 44
8.5 Long-term reliability 49
8.6 Preparation of report 50

9 References **51**

Appendix A: model specification of a supplementary load test **52**

Appendix B: measurement of existing stresses **55**

Appendix C: risk analysis **59**

Appendix D: case studies **64**

1 Introduction

1.1 Background

It is well known that there are reserves of strength in many highway and railway bridges, particularly the older ones which are difficult to evaluate by the usual analytical methods. This problem has been highlighted by the current programme of highway bridge assessment and strengthening which has revealed a large number of bridges which seem to be carrying normal traffic in a satisfactory manner, with no undue signs of distress, but failed their assessments. It is felt by many practising engineers that a better idea of the capacity of such bridges could be gained by observing their behaviour under the application of known loads which are representative of the loads they are likely to carry in practice.

Load testing is in fact used in several countries both to evaluate the load-bearing capacity of existing bridges and to validate the design of new constructions before they go into service. This document, which is based on a distillation of current experience, provides guidelines for the use of supplementary load testing in the evaluation of the safe load capacity of suitable highway and railway bridges. It provides a framework for deciding whether or not load testing should be considered as well as practical advice on its application and the safe and consistent interpretation of the results.

1.2 Forms of static load testing

Load tests are usually undertaken to investigate the adequacy or otherwise of the bridge superstructure rather than the sub-structure or foundations, although in some forms of structure these are interlinked. In addition, load testing can be used to monitor the condition of structures which are known to be deteriorating or which have undergone a major structural repair or strengthening. The main forms of static load testing are described below.

1.2.1 Supplementary load tests

Supplementary load tests, as their name suggests, are intended to supplement the analytical methods of assessment based on calculation and the use of codes of practice. The results from such tests provide an indication of how the structure is actually behaving under load and how the loads are being distributed through the various structural members. This information can then be used to modify the mathematical model representing the structure so that the results obtained from analyses more closely conform to those obtained from the load test. Supplementary load tests are thus not used in isolation to determine the capacity of a structure, but are very much part of the whole assessment procedure. The levels of loading necessary are such that they will be sufficient to obtain satisfactory measurable responses from the structure concerned without causing any permanent structural damage. It is unlikely that such loading will exceed the loads experienced by the structure under normal traffic.

1.2.2 Proof loading

Proof loading is normally undertaken on newly constructed bridges that are novel and/or safety critical, in order to validate the design method and the various design assumptions. A proof load test is therefore intended to show that the design and construction have been carried out in a satisfactory manner rather than trying to prove the load-carrying capacity of the structure. As such proof loading is especially valuable where new design concepts or new materials are being used. In many respects proof loading is similar to supplementary load testing in that the test results are used to check or amend the theoretical analysis. The main difference is that the level of the proof loading is likely to be higher than that used in supplementary tests and is generally equivalent to the level of loading specified for the serviceability limit state. Proof load testing is seldom used in the UK because of the confidence in modern methods of analysis and the availability of comprehensive design codes based on the latest research.

1.2.3 Proving load testing

Proving load testing has similar objectives to supplementary load testing in that it is used to provide a more realistic evaluation of the safe load-carrying capacity of a structure than that obtained from theoretical analysis alone. The main difference is that the proving load test results are used directly to derive a safe load-carrying capacity without any further theoretical analysis. During the test, the load is increased in increments to some predetermined maximum or until the structure shows signs of deterioration or distress. The safe load-carrying capacity is then derived from the maximum test load by reducing it by an appropriate load factor. Proving load tests can therefore require considerably higher levels of loading than used in the other forms of testing and this increases the risk that the structure may be irreversibly damaged. The use of proving load testing within the UK is the subject of a current review by the National Steering Committee – Bridge Testing in association with the Highways Agency (HA). Advice on such tests will be given at a later date.

1.2.4 Dynamic load testing

Dynamic load testing, using either ambient or forced vibrations, is another form of load testing which is used to evaluate the performance of a structure. The results, which are usually a measure of stiffness rather than strength, may be used to validate the predictions of design calculations or, alternatively, a comparison of results over time may be used to monitor any deterioration or serious damage to the structure. It is possible to estimate structural properties from the results of dynamic testing and so provide a check on the assumptions made in any theoretical analysis. However, dynamic testing is only likely to be useful on those structures which are fairly responsive to dynamic loading. It should be noted that moving vehicles can generate dynamic loading on a bridge deck without causing a significant dynamic response in the structure itself.

1.3 Scope of guidelines

This report provides guidelines on the use of supplementary load testing carried out as an integral part of the overall assessment procedure. The principles set out in the guidelines can be applied to any type of structure which is amenable to theoretical analysis and which can be dealt with under the current assessment procedures. However, the practical problems of applying sufficient live test loading to longer span structures means that the main application will be for small- to medium-span structures. The guidelines are not material specific, but some of the instrumentation techniques will be more suitable for one type of material than another. Moreover, the guidelines are more likely to be applied to older structures, where there is greater uncertainty about their structural behaviour due to outdated forms of construction, or, because the structural details are not known.

Due to the largely empirical methods used to assess the carrying capacity of masonry arches, the guidelines cannot be applied directly to this form of construction (Page, 1994). However, some guidance is given in Section 2.6 on the use of test loading as an aid to monitoring the condition of such structures.

The guidelines cover the use of supplementary load testing for the assessment of both complete structures and particular components of the structure which may be critical in determining the capacity of the structure as a whole. Not all types of structure or structural component are suitable for load testing because of possible brittle modes of failure. Load tests on live structures can be expensive to carry out, with considerable indirect costs for traffic management etc., and the benefits of such tests need to be carefully evaluated before any decision to undertake a test is made. The guidelines provide a framework for the assessing engineer to help him or her in making such a decision for particular structures. Because of the link with the analytical assessment method the guidelines must be used in conjunction with the current assessment documentation in order to arrive at a safe load bearing capacity for a structure.

The guidelines contain practical information on the planning and execution of a load test. Information is given about the different types of instrumentation that are available and the methods of recording and interpreting the data. Some examples of structures where supplementary load testing has been used in the assessment process are included in Appendix D.

Supplementary load testing uses the 'real' structure as a model and whilst such testing often gives the engineer confidence that the structural system strength is much higher than the initial assessment value, this should be treated with caution. The disadvantage of using the 'real' structure is that it can be difficult to separate out the influence of the different effects contributing to the overall response. It is necessary therefore to be sure that the different effects that could be contributing to the system strength are fully identified and understood, especially those which may be of a brittle or transient nature. Typical examples are seized bearings and the composite action of fill or surfacing material. Some beneficial effects cannot be relied on over time or at the ultimate limit state without modification to the structure. Generally there will be more confidence placed on those additional sources of strength where there is some physical feature of the structure which ensures that they are always mobilized.

The location and types of measurement adopted for any test must be examined critically with respect to location and the condition of the structure. The proximity of defects such as cracking, yielding, delamination, etc. can all affect measurements considerably and not necessarily consistently. The results could, for example, indicate low stress in a member when the converse might be the true situation.

Supplementary load testing is likely to be most effective when the structure is known to contain features which are difficult to model by theoretical analysis, but which can contribute to the load-carrying capacity.

To help the assessing engineer determine whether supplementary load testing is likely to be of assistance in the assessment of a particular structure the various steps in the use of supplementary load testing within the overall assessment process are given below with references to the relevant sections of the document. This is summarized in Figures 1.1 and 1.2.

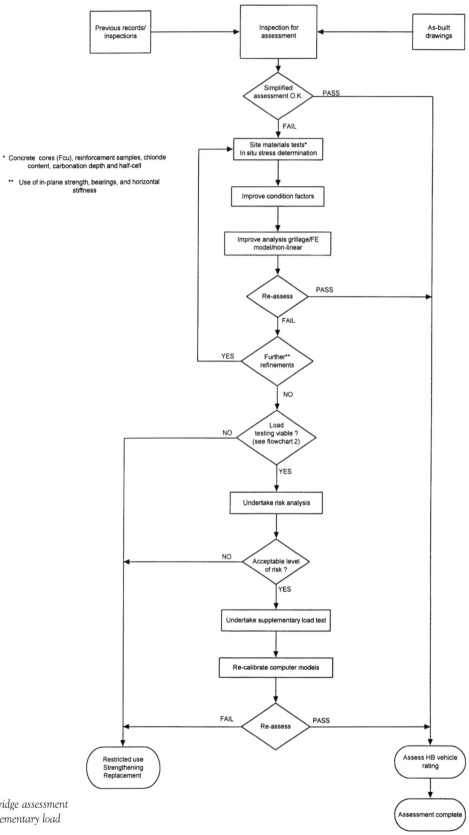

* Concrete cores (Fcu), reinforcement samples, chloride content, carbonation depth and half-cell

** Use of in-plane strength, bearings, and horizontal stiffness

Figure 1.1 Bridge assessment including supplementary load tests.

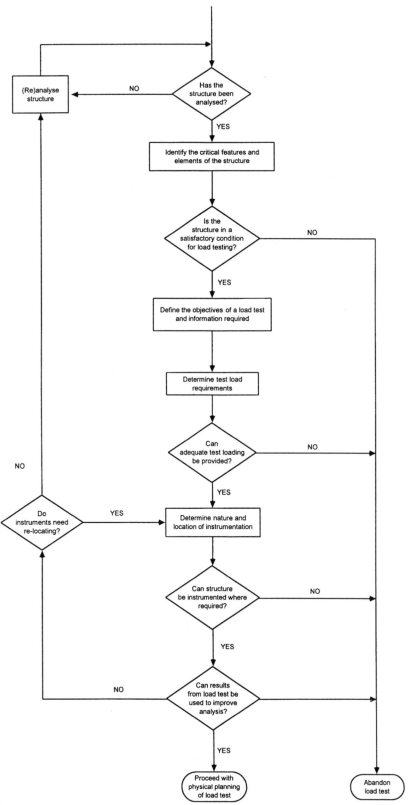

Figure 1.2   Supplementary load testing – feasibility study.

1.4 Use of guidelines

These guidelines are applicable to a wide variety of structural forms, methods of construction and construction materials. They are intended to be used by the experienced practitioner with expertise in the field of load testing and also provide information for client organizations who may be considering load testing proposals.

Step 1. If the structure has been inspected, the Engineer should check that the report is recent and visit the site to confirm that nothing has changed or been missed. The Engineer should be satisfied that available drawings accurately represent the present structure.

Step 2. Carry out an initial theoretical assessment of the structure to determine its safe load-carrying capacity. The assessment process and the relevance of supplementary load testing are discussed in Chapter 2. In particular, note should be taken of Section 2.5 which considers the role of supplementary load testing in improving the understanding of the behaviour of the structure under load.

Step 3. From the results of the assessment determine which are the members which are critical in determining the load-carrying capacity of the structure. Decide whether a more sophisticated method of analysis or a re-evaluation of member strengths might be beneficial (see Section 2.8).

Step 4. Determine whether the results of a load test are likely to help in enhancing the calculated load-carrying capacity of the structure. The features of a structure and aspects of structural behaviour which are amenable to investigation by load testing are described in Section 3.3. For shortfall in shear capacity see Section 3.1.

Step 5. Identify the objectives of a possible load test (see Section 2.1). This must include the effects which are to be measured and their locations. In addition consideration should be given to the level of loading that is likely to be required, whether it can be safely applied, and its location.

Step 6. Carry out a desk-top feasibility study to see whether, from a technical point of view, load testing is feasible. The various stages in such a study are given in Section 3.4 with Figure 1.2.

Step 7. Plan the technical details of the load test including the locations of the measuring instruments and the type and positions of the applied loading. Any traffic management requirements which affect the time or method of testing should be taken into account (see Chapter 4). The different methods of load application are discussed in Chapter 5. The various types of equipment for measuring deflections, strains, etc. are described in Chapter 6.

Step 8. Calculate the response to loading to enable the maximum test load to be set. Deflections and strains should be calculated with sufficient accuracy to enable the locations and ranges of the instruments to be selected.

Step 9. Carry out a risk analysis which takes account of the possibility of the structure being damaged during the test and the consequences of such damage (see Section 4.6). A form of risk analysis is given in Appendix C. Although such a risk analysis may indicate that in some cases load testing should not be considered, in general the objective is to indicate the level of experience and expertise which is required in the particular case.

Step 10. Estimate the cost of the load test and decide whether it is cost effective in the light of alternative courses of action.

Step 11. Plan the practical and operational details of the test itself. This will include the installation of the instrumentation, the loading procedures, staffing requirements and duties, traffic management, liaison with other bodies, and emergency procedures (see Chapter 7).

Step 12. Carry out the load test including any preliminary site work and the setting up of equipment (see Sections 7.3 and 7.4). Apply the loading and measure the various responses (see Sections 7.5 and 7.6) and compare with calculated values.

Step 13. Interpret the results from the load test to determine a revised evaluation of the load-carrying capacity of the structure (see Chapter 8). The results may be used either to modify the structural idealization used in the analysis of the structure or to determine the nature and extent of other forms of structural action which are being mobilized to resist the applied loads. It will be necessary to evaluate the long-term reliability of some effects which are found to be contributing to the load resistance (see Section 8.5). Any unusual or alarming results should be reported to the client or owner as soon as possible.

Step 14. Prepare a report on the load test (see Section 8.6). In general, the test report and findings will be incorporated in a comprehensive report on the assessment of the structure which will include recommendations about its safe load-bearing capacity.

Model specification. A model specification for a load test to be carried out as part of the assessment of a structure is given in Appendix A.

2 The assessment process

2.1 Objectives and procedures

The main objective of a structural assessment is to determine the load that a given structure can carry with a reasonable probability that it will not suffer serious damage so as to endanger any persons or property on or near the structure. It should be noted, however, that structural assessments are valid only at the time they are carried out and do not take into account future deterioration. In the case of public road bridges, the loading capacity is normally determined in relation to the loading possible from any convoy of vehicles permitted under the current vehicle Construction and Use regulations (Road Vehicles (Construction and Use) Regulations, 1986) including allowances for overloading and the dynamic behaviour of the vehicles. Where the full loading cannot be carried it is necessary to determine a safe lower level of loading which can be linked to weight restrictions based on easily identified vehicle types. Because of the uncertainties involved in predicting the maximum loads that a bridge could experience during the course of its lifetime, and because of uncertainties over the future deterioration of the structure, there must be some margin of safety built into the assessment process.

In general, bridge structures in the UK are assessed by the application of limit state principles, although there are exceptions for cast iron and masonry structures. It is also usual to carry out the assessment for the ultimate limit state only, since assessments are carried out for reasons of safety rather than to ensure durability. The use of analytical methods similar to the approach adopted for design allows the safe ultimate load capacity of a structure to be calculated directly but may give an unusually low strength.

The assessment procedure, as in design, is normally element or component based in that it is the ability of individual elements to resist various load effects that is investigated. The load effects, such as bending moments and shear forces, are determined from the different load cases by some form of analysis where the structure is modelled in mathematical terms. The appropriate strengths or resistances of the different elements to the different types of load effect are obtained from an appropriate national standard. The verification of structural adequacy will include partial safety factors on both the load and resistance sides of the equations to ensure that a defined margin of safety is built into the process. This safety margin has to allow for factors which cannot be known at the time, such as grossly overloaded vehicles and undetected deterioration of the structure. There is then a reasonable probability that, providing the structure remains in its current condition, it will continue to be able to function safely.

2.2 Inspection

The assessment of a structure for its load-carrying capacity involves not only analysis and calculation, but also a comprehensive inspection of the structure concerned. Such an inspection is necessary to verify the form of construction, the dimensions of the structure and its components and their general condition. An inspection will note any signs of deterioration and deficiencies such as cracking, corrosion, settlement, defective bearings, etc. Information about the structure which might be relevant to an assessment can be obtained from as-built drawings, site records, material records and inspection reports, and consultation with statutory undertakers.

Information about the presence of utilities is important and can be obtained both from observations made during the site visit, a trial excavation and/or consultation with the utility companies. The presence of utilities can affect the assessment of the structure. If present they can significantly add to superimposed dead load and damage may have been done during installation, leaving the structure weaker than expected. Cases of trenches cut through crowns of arches and fixings drilled through tendons or reinforcement are not unknown.

Much of the information gathered in the inspection will be useful in deciding whether or not to undertake a supplementary load test. For instance, cracking at the supports could be indicative of inadequate shear resistance and hence predispose against load testing because of the brittle nature of shear failures. Information on the performance of the bearings may provide a clue as to whether some additional restraint was present which could affect the load-carrying capacity and which may be revealed by a load test. Information derived from construction records will be helpful in determining the sequence of construction and hence what dead load stresses might have been developed within the various members.

Although the available inspection information may be adequate for making a decision about load testing, it may be necessary to carry out a further inspection especially if the structure has serious defects. If it is then decided to undertake a load test, the additional information obtained will be useful for deciding the testing required, and the procedures for carrying it out.

2.3 Materials

For the purposes of assessment it is necessary to assume values for the properties of the construction materials. Initial assessments may well be based on nominal values given in the national standards which are appropriate for the age of the material. More realistic values can be found from testing or from reference to construction records, and these could well be higher than the nominal values. The assessment procedures now allow the adoption of worst credible values. Thus within the assessment process there is scope for improving the calculated strength of elements by adopting more realistic and higher values for the relevant material properties.

The strengths of the materials are important factors in calculating the resistances of the load-bearing elements that determine the capacity of the structure as a whole. Thus the yield stress of the steel is an important factor in determining the strength of a stiffened plate panel; the compressive strength of concrete will have a significant influence on the moment of resistance of a reinforced concrete beam. However, these critical material properties will have little influence on the behaviour of a structure which is significantly below its collapse load. Load testing in this range which does not cause irreversible damage to the structure can only yield information about the stiffness of the structure and its components, whereas to determine collapse loads requires a knowledge of the strengths of the structure and its components. However, the material properties concerned with elastic behaviour are an implicit part of the response of any structure under load, although they cannot of course be identified from the load test results.

While a precise knowledge of the properties of the materials in a structure is essential for the analytical process, it is not so important for the load testing itself or for the interpretation of the results. However, some knowledge of the properties could be useful in deciding whether or not to carry out a load test at all. For instance, the identification of a brittle material such as cast iron would put a question mark over the possibility of load testing because of the danger of a sudden collapse. In some cases the absolute values of moduli of elasticity are less important than the ratio of the moduli in the longitudinal and transverse directions.

2.4 Loading

The loading used for assessment purposes is specified in the assessment codes together with the methods of application (*Design Manual for Roads and Bridges* 3.4, 1998).

Within the assessment procedure there is the possibility of adopting a lower level of loading if it can be justified by the particular circumstances of the structure concerned. For instance, if the surface of a road bridge and its approaches is very smooth there could be a case for reducing the allowance for impact built into the loading. In the case of a long-span structure carrying a low percentage of heavy goods vehicles, a loading derived specifically for that bridge could well be lighter than the full nominal loading.

2.5 Analysis of the structure

Analysis of the structure is an important part of the assessment process since, in many cases, it is the lack of understanding about the behaviour of the real structure which makes it difficult to predict a 'true' value for the safe load-bearing capacity of the bridge. Most assessments will start with a fairly simple method of analysis, and will only progress to a more complex method if the structure fails the assessment. However, the accuracy of the assessment does not depend only on the sophistication of the computer program being used, but also on the accuracy with which the structure is modelled. This means that not only do the stiffnesses of the various elements need to be correctly represented, but that boundary restraints and joint fixities must also be given proper values at both the serviceability and ultimate limit states. While it may be possible to calculate some of these parameters fairly accurately for the basic structure, there may be some difficulty in doing so when there are non-structural appendages which affect the overall structural behaviour. For instance, continuous surfacing across a simply supported end joint may provide some kind of rotational restraint; surfacing can act compositely with the deck to increase the bending stiffness of the structure. Another area of uncertainty in structural modelling can be in estimating the area over which a concentrated load is dispersed through the structure.

In the analysis part of the assessment process two sorts of improvement are possible:

- more sophisticated methods of analysis can be used which model more closely the configurations of the structure, such as the use of a three-dimensional finite element program rather than a two-dimensional grillage to model the behaviour of a beam and slab type deck
- the quality of the data fed into the analytical model can be improved by basing the values on actual test results rather than conservative assumptions.

Generally, elastic methods are used to obtain the load distributions which are assumed to be relevant for the ultimate limit state. These will be lower bound or safe solutions and so may underestimate the true collapse capacity of the structure. However, elastic methods allow the results from different load cases to be superimposed and this means that the stiffnesses of the members do not have to be recalculated each time there is a load increment. In certain circumstances non-linear methods can be used when investigating the response of particular complex components, for example when calculating the strength of discretely stiffened steel panels. For slab-type bridges, yield line methods of analysis are available which consider the state of the complete structure at the point of collapse. These methods can give a better estimate of the collapse strength of the structure, but they are upper bound methods which can lead to unsafe solutions if the yield line pattern is not correctly identified. It should be noted that most design and assessment procedures are concerned with checking that individual elements and components are adequate rather than considering the adequacy of the structure as a whole.

All structures have to carry their own dead weight as well as other superimposed dead loads due to surfacing, parapets, etc. The effects of these loads on the different members have to be determined and in some cases this can be a fairly straightforward task because the uniformly distributed nature of the loads requires very little sophisticated analysis. However, there are other 'load effects' present in an unloaded structure which may have come from, say, the settlement of a support in a continuous structure or from the prestressing forces applied to a prestressed concrete beam. The determination of these residual effects is important as they affect the amount of resistance in a member which is available at the time to resist the live loading. Creep or corrosion effects may cause some uncertainty over the value of these residual effects and the stresses they cause. These residual stresses may therefore need to be determined when carrying out a load test, although they may well have been already determined as part of the assessment process. Methods for determining residual stresses in steel and concrete elements are discussed in Appendix B.

In the case of cast-iron structures very little extrapolation is required because their assessments are based on permissible stresses which are of the same order as those that are likely to be produced during any supplementary load test. For other materials the accuracy of the derived analytical models at higher loads will depend to some extent on what factors have been taken into account in the revision of the models. In general, the contributing factors are more favourable transverse distribution, composite action between structural elements such as beams and non-structural fill material and surfacing, and restraints at the supports. The latter can include both torsional and longitudinal in-plane restraint. In considering the applicability of the improved analytical model at the ultimate limit state it may be thought wise to reduce the contributions of some or all of the factors. This will be discussed further in Section 8.4. It should be noted that there is a difference between structural behaviour which may be modified as a result of moving from serviceability to ultimate or collapse conditions and behaviour which may be modified because of the passage of time.

2.6 Masonry and concrete arches

Masonry arch bridges are infilled structures and the internal dimensions of haunching, buttresses and spandrel wall thicknesses are often not available. In addition to this the interaction between the structure and fill is not fully understood. It is therefore, difficult to apply supplementary load-testing techniques to masonry arch bridges because the assessment techniques are largely empirical. More rigorous methods are available using mechanism or finite element programs which can result in an improved capacity, but it is unlikely to be improved by a supplementary load test. The problem with masonry arches is that they behave structurally in a complex manner but have weak areas that could suffer damage during a test. Serious defects in masonry arches result from failure of the bond between components which then allows them to behave as independent structures (Melbourne, 1990). For example, under heavy loading the arch barrel will tend to detach from the spandrels either by breaking the joint between them or by a fracture through the arch ring itself. Also, most masonry arch rings are only bonded to each other by a mortar bed and the interfacial shear between the rings under loading can cause ring separation. Both of these defects can occur well below the ultimate load and whilst many arches in this condition continue to perform well, it is not advisable to conduct a test at load levels that may initiate a fracture which could affect the future serviceability of the structure.

Research on railway arches by Broomhead and Clark (1994) and Clark (1995) found that when an arch suffers regular loading sufficient to cause a stress in the barrel of approximately half the ultimate stress of the masonry, a rapid serviceability failure can follow. The research was carried out as a result of an observed increase in the rate of serviceability failure in arches subject to 25-tonne axle load freight traffic. It was also found that where the masonry was saturated the life of the structure was further reduced. These findings are not surprising because at the ultimate load, arches form a hinged mechanism with cracking and crushing of the masonry, ring separation and large displacements of the barrel. From collapse testing it is apparent that many of these defects are initiated at loadings significantly below that necessary for collapse and if the normal traffic causes loading of this magnitude, a serviceability failure will result.

The research findings indicate an approach that a bridge owner could use to conduct a load test on a masonry arch that would give an indication of the likelihood of serviceability failure under current traffic. It could not determine a safe assessment loading in itself, excepting that if the risk of a serviceability failure is proved remote then the ultimate loading will be considerably higher.

It is recommended, therefore, that load tests on masonry arches are carried out only after conducting flat jack tests to determine the dead load stresses in the arch barrel (Building Research Establishment, 1995). The results from these tests then need to be carefully analysed to establish how the arch is behaving before proceeding. It has been found by Harvey (1995) that the stresses are often higher than expected at the springing, but lower than expected at the crown. This indicates that the abutments have spread slightly under load and the bridge is behaving as a three-hinged arch. This is to be expected and it is likely that many arches are in this condition as a result of the initial deflection that occurred when the centring was removed.

Providing that the inspection records show that the arch is not suffering a progressive increase in defects and the dead load stresses are determined, the arch barrel can be instrumented and tested under a loading known to be within the existing traffic loads. If the strains recorded indicate that total stresses in areas of the arch barrel are approaching half the ultimate stress in the masonry, there is a high risk that a serviceability failure may occur. However, in the short term, the ultimate strength of the bridge is likely to be adequate.

Many of the reservations discussed above do not apply to concrete arches. They are a comparatively rare form of construction that, depending on the amount and positioning of reinforcement, can suffer from similar defects to masonry. Concrete arches are, however, much less tolerant of ground movements and unless constructed as a three-pinned design are likely to develop cracks in the arch barrel. While concrete arches can be instrumented and tested, they are usually very strong structures and any tests are likely to be related to the behaviour under load of specific details or defects.

2.7 Strength of members

An important part of the assessment process is checking the ability of the various structural members to resist the load effects, including dead and live load effects, derived from the analysis. This is usually done by reference to a relevant national design code, but there are important differences between design and assessment. In assessment the actual dimensions of the elements, based on site measurements, can be used with due allowances for corrosion and other deterioration. More realistic values of material properties can be used based either on test samples or on supplier's certificates. In some cases the assessing engineer can deduce a worst credible strength from several sources of information and this may be combined with the use of lower partial factors. In the case of steel members the actual initial deformations due to manufacture can be measured and used in calculations.

These ideas have been incorporated, along with other relaxations, in the development of assessment versions of the main national design codes for steel and concrete. The intention is to achieve a more realistic estimate of the strength of the structural elements based on their actual properties and so eliminate some of the conservatism which is necessarily built into design codes to cater for a wide range of as yet unbuilt structures. In design codes there is the inevitable rounding-off of values and the adoption of lower bounds to experimental results. There may be sharp cut-offs for certain parameters with no way of interpolating for those cases which do not quite comply. In steel codes there are usually built-in values for such parameters as residual stresses and initial deformations which can significantly affect the calculated strength and stiffness of the element concerned. The assessment versions of the codes provide the information necessary to calculate the strength of the elements using the actual, rather than assumed, values for parameters. Assessment codes also provide guidance for dealing with details which have gone out of fashion and are no longer covered by current codes. Assessment versions of design codes are an effective way of obtaining more realistic estimates for the strength/capacity of individual elements in real-life structures.

In load testing, many of the variations discussed above are automatically taken into account since the test is carried out on the structure as it actually exists. But, of course, some of the parameters only become significant as the element or structure approaches collapse. Since the aim is to avoid damage to the structure it is unlikely that the results from load testing alone can be used to improve the estimate of member strengths.

2.8 Treatment of structures that do not meet the requirements of the assessment codes

The previous discussions have highlighted some ways to improve the load capacity of a structure which fails its initial assessment. The subsequent action taken by the assessing engineer will depend on a number of factors such as the extent of the shortfall in load capacity, the nature of any faults, the general condition of the structure and its response under traffic. It may be desirable to repeat the assessment using more realistic material properties, a more sophisticated form of analysis and/or using assessment versions of design codes for calculating element strengths. In many cases these steps may be sufficient to pass the structure for its full loading. In other cases the bridge owner may opt to install temporary supports or adopt some bridge management strategy such as reducing the number of traffic lanes or imposing weight restrictions.

The various improvements in the assessment process outlined above can be achieved at little cost as they involve mainly desk studies. These are therefore likely to be undertaken before any thought is given to load testing. However, if it is an important structure which is fairly complex there may well be a case for seeking to improve the structural modelling used in the analysis by seeing how the structure behaves under known loadings. Thus, load testing becomes another option for dealing with structures that have failed assessment. It is likely to be an expensive option having an element of risk which will need careful consideration before it is undertaken. There is also the risk of the structure being assessed at too high a capacity due to the use of load-test-derived enhancements which may be transient, for example, the sudden loss of composite or membrane action or boundary restraint as the loading approaches the assessed value.

It should be remembered that any bridge in service is undergoing some form of load test several times a day and observations and some measurements taken in such a situation may provide invaluable information which will allow the assessing engineer to make a confident decision about its future.

2.9   Summary

Current assessment procedures are similar to the procedures followed in the design of new structures. However, there is a certain amount of additional conservatism built into the design of notional and as yet unbuilt structures which needs to be removed if the true load-carrying capacity of a particular bridge is to be found. Some of the relaxations which can be adopted in assessment have been discussed in this chapter. One of the crucial factors in determining the load-carrying capacity is the manner in which the applied loads are distributed through the structure and are resisted by the various elements forming that structure. This may be fairly easy to establish in the case of new design for the basic structure, but the structural behaviour may be more difficult to understand for existing, and particularly older, structures where the addition of non-structural appendages can significantly affect structural behaviour.

The method of construction may also not be amenable to the form of modelling necessary when using modern analytical methods. For instance, in the case of a deck consisting of masonry jack arches spanning transversely between longitudinal steel beams it may be very difficult to estimate the value of the effective transverse stiffness of the deck even though the way that the loads are transferred is easy to understand.

Supplementary load testing using a loading applied in the elastic range provides a way of gaining a better understanding of the behaviour of a structure and of obtaining more realistic values for the parameters that need to be included in any method of analysis. Supplementary load testing is thus part of the assessment process and is not an activity which on its own can lead to the determination of load-carrying capacities. It will not provide the answer in every case where apparently satisfactory structures fail their initial assessment and there will be restrictions on its use.

3 Use of supplementary load testing

3.1 Introduction

Load testing provides a way of determining how a real structure actually behaves under the applied loading. In a way load testing can be seen as the analogue counterpart of the digitized methods used in most forms of structural modelling, except that the load test is done on an exact full-sized model. A disadvantage of using the 'real' structure as a model is that it is often difficult to separate the influence of the different effects which contribute to the overall response. However, supplementary load testing does provide a way of improving the accuracy of the mathematical model used in structural analysis so that it more closely models the behaviour of the real structure.

This chapter provides guidance on whether supplementary load testing is likely to be a suitable and useful option within the assessment process. It is assumed that at least an initial inspection and assessment will have been carried out and the structure shown to be incapable of carrying the required loading. The initial assessment will have identified the weaknesses in the structure which are responsible for determining the calculated load-carrying capacity. In many cases some degree of re-analysis using revised material properties or assessment versions of design codes will have been carried out but without increasing the load-carrying capacity sufficiently to allow the structure to 'pass'.

The aim of supplementary load testing is to produce measurable elastic deformation to the structure, such as deflection or surface strain, without causing permanent damage.

The suitability of a structure for load testing will depend on the following factors:

- the possibility of developing a more realistic analytical model for structural behaviour based on measured rather than theoretical values of stiffness parameters
- the possibility of mobilizing structural actions which are not considered during a normal theoretical analysis but which can contribute to load-carrying capacity
- the risk of the structure being damaged or even collapsing during the test
- the ductility of the structure and the ability to measure its response under normal traffic loading
- whether the structure is of a type that would give adequate warning of impending damage.

The question of risk and its management will be dealt with in Chapter 4 where it will be linked to the level of competence and care required to carry out the test in the particular circumstances. The present chapter will consider the first two factors and look at certain aspects of structural behaviour which are likely to be better understood and quantified as the result of load testing and which will lead to a more realistic evaluation of the load-carrying capacity of the structure.

Load testing is not recommended when the deficiencies affect the shear or bearing capacity at a support. Apart from the fact that most shear failures occur suddenly and without warning, maximum shears usually occur at or near to supports where even on soft bearings the deflections and rotations are going to be small. Thus, even under fairly high levels of loading there will be little to measure which could give an indication of the shears being carried by the detail and there are, in fact, no techniques at present available for monitoring and determining the shear stresses in a section.

3.2 Condition of structure

An important consideration before undertaking any load testing is the condition of the structure as a whole, including the state of the supports, and the state of the various components. It would be unwise to consider testing a structure where there were signs of extensive deterioration such as crumbling concrete or heavily corroded steel sections. Similarly it would be unwise to consider testing a structure which already had significant deflections under both dead and live load or where there were significant cracks in critical locations. Load testing is primarily aimed at identifying and quantifying additional sources of strength in structures which are showing little if any signs of weakness or distress under normal traffic.

When considering the state of the structure, note should be taken of any repairs that have been carried out in the past and which might affect the structural behaviour. Trenches dug through the road surfacing to maintain buried services could affect the dispersion of concentrated loads through the surfacing and underlying fill.

3.3 Structural action

Supplementary load testing is likely to be most effective when the structure is known to contain features which are difficult to model by theoretical analysis but which can contribute to the load-carrying capacity. For instance older types of construction using discrete longitudinal beams may rely upon mechanisms for transverse load distribution. For longitudinal beams which are shaped in the form of a shallow arch there will be some arching action under load if the ends are restrained which can supplement the normal bending resistance of the beams. Thus, an important part of any decision-making process considering supplementary load testing should be a careful evaluation of the behaviour of the structure concerned and an identification of the various load-bearing mechanisms which are being mobilized. This study should seek to identify those mechanisms which are amenable to analytical methods and those where load testing might help to quantify their effectiveness.

3.3.1 Transverse load distribution

Doubts about the effectiveness of transverse load distribution mechanisms or about how much of the structure is providing resistance to a particular form of load or action can often be resolved by some form of load testing. For instance, in older types of construction, with masonry jack arches or metal buckle plates spanning between longitudinal girders, it is very difficult to calculate the contribution of the transverse elements to the transverse stiffness of the structure. In this case, load testing provides the only way of obtaining a true value for the stiffness parameter for inclusion in an analysis. A similar situation occurs in decks made from discrete longitudinal beams which rely on some form of shear connection or on transverse prestressing to provide the mechanism for the transverse distribution of the loading. A suitable case for investigation by load testing would be transverse load distribution where the transverse stiffness parameters are not amenable to calculation or where there is some doubt over the effectiveness of the medium providing the transverse continuity (see Figures 3.1 and 3.2).

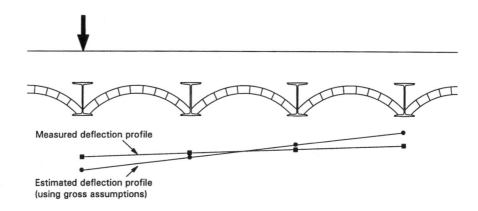

(a) Steel girders and masonry jack arches

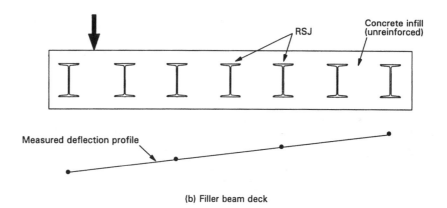

Figure 3.1   Examples where estimations of transverse stiffness properties of the deck is not readily available to calculation.

(b) Filler beam deck

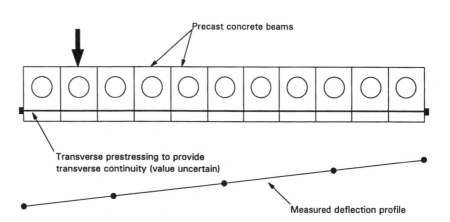

Figure 3.2   An example of situations where effectiveness of the transverse load distribution is uncertain.

3.3.2 Composite action

Another source of uncertainty is the extent to which composite action is taking place between different components of a structure which may not have been specifically designed with this form of structural action in mind. In steel trough decks with concrete infill but with no recognized form of shear connection it will be difficult to calculate the extent to which the friction between the concrete and the steel is encouraging some degree of composite action. A similar situation can arise in all concrete bridges where contiguous concrete beams are covered with a layer of in situ concrete. If there are no physical connections such as shear links between the beams and the in situ concrete fill it will be difficult to estimate the extent to which the roughness of the interface can lead to composite action. In both cases the extent to which composite action was taking place could be quantified by observing the strain pattern developing across a vertical section of the deck as it was loaded. Any analysis could then be modified accordingly (see Figure 3.3).

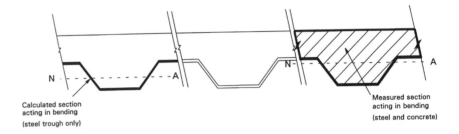

(a) Steel trough deck and concrete infill

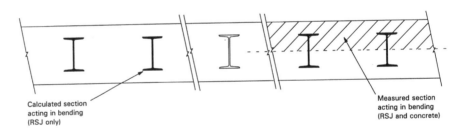

(b) Filler joist deck

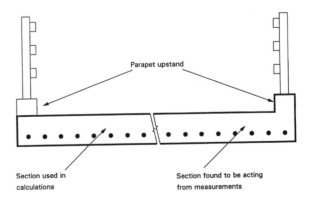

(c) Concrete deck with upstands

Figure 3.3 Examples of 'undesigned' composite action.

3.3.3 Boundary restraints

Another important influence on overall structural behaviour is the type and level of restraint applied at the boundaries of the structure. In the case of simply supported structures it is generally assumed that there is only vertical restraint and that any friction from the bearings can be ignored. But continuous surfacing over buried joints or friction in the bearings can provide some rotational and translational restraint which affects the response of the structure and increases its load bearing capacity. Here again load testing provides a method for quantifying these effects. Examples of the different forms of restraint encountered are shown in Figures 3.4 and 3.5.

3.3.4 Pin-joint fixity

Suitable details for load testing include those where there is some uncertainty about the actual restraints or boundary conditions which are effective at the ends of the member in question. Thus in supposedly pin-jointed truss members there will undoubtedly be some form of restraint which can improve the resistance of the member against buckling under compression. In the case of a three-girder steel bridge with transverse cross-girders it is often assumed for design that the connections to the

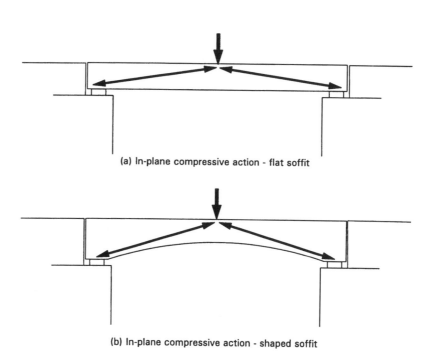

(a) In-plane compressive action - flat soffit

(b) In-plane compressive action - shaped soffit

Figure 3.4   Restraint at the end of longitudinal members mobilizing in-plane compressive forces.

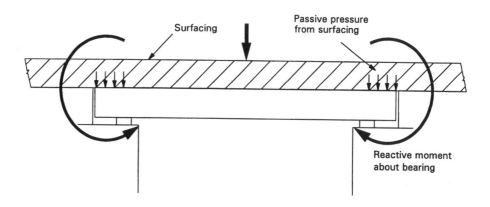

Figure 3.5   Resistance moments from supports from continuous testing.

outer girders are pin jointed, but the connection across the central girder is fixed. A load test on a cross-girder would give an indication of the magnitude of any fixity at the free end and allow the calculated bending resistance of the cross-girder to be enhanced accordingly.

3.3.5 Transverse compression

In the case of a concentrated load applied to the concrete deck slab of a beam-and-slab-type bridge, in-plane compressive forces can be generated which provide additional resistance to the load together with the normal bending and shear resistance (see Figure 3.6). The presence of this effect can be verified by load testing and to some extent quantified. If the overall carrying capacity of the structure is determined by its ability to resist local loads then a verifying load test could be restricted to the area in question and would be carried out differently from a global test.

3.4 Feasibility study

In order to decide whether or not to undertake a load test in a particular situation it will be necessary to undertake a feasibility study which should include the following steps:

(a) Identify from earlier analyses and inspections those features or elements of the structure that have the potential to enhance the assessed capacity.

(b) Check that the structure as a whole and the relevant details are in a reasonable physical condition, noting any excessive deflections or signs of serious and significant corrosion.

(c) Define in detail the objectives of a possible load test. This should be in general terms such as an improved understanding of structural behaviour as well as specific information such as the identification of strength enhancing parameters and their means of evaluation.

(d) Determine the levels and location of loading required to meet the objectives in (c) above. The level of loading must be sufficient to produce measurable displacements and strains without causing irreversible damage.

(e) Determine the measurements necessary to meet the objectives in (c) above. This will include both the type of measurement to be recorded and the location of the instruments on the structure.

(f) Check that it will be possible to provide and install the loading and instrumentation identified in (d) and (e) above. For example, on long structures it might be difficult to provide enough load to successfully carry out a test. Similarly the form of construction of a bridge or its location might make it difficult to install the measuring instruments in the required positions.

(g) Confirm that the results obtained from the load test can be used in the analytical process to derive a revised estimate of the load-carrying capacity of the structure. The main objective of a supplementary load test is to improve the analytical model by calibrating it against the measured responses. There must therefore be

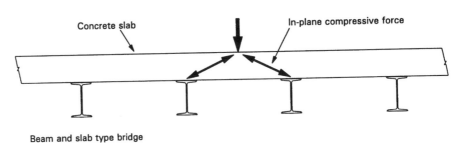

Figure 3.6   Example of the development of local in-plane compressive forces.

a suitable analytical model to allow this to be done. If the original analysis has been a simple one, based, say, on published distribution factors, it may not be possible to modify these in the light of the load test results; it will then be necessary to undertake a more sophisticated form of analysis.

It is important in considering the possibility of a load test that full account is taken of the applicability and benefit of the information to be derived from the tests. There may be some doubt about the long-term reliability of some of the effects which are modifying the structural behaviour, but this does not mean that a load test is not worthwhile. In some cases it may be enough to know that there is a reserve of strength which, even though it may reduce with time, will still provide confidence that the structure can safely be allowed to remain in service.

One factor which might affect the feasibility of carrying out a load test is the physical amount of load that might be necessary to produce the required results. Although the level of loading is likely to be lower than that experienced by the structure from everyday traffic it might nevertheless prove to be difficult to provide and handle that level of loading in a static test. This is likely to be a problem when investigating overall load distribution in longer span structures.

Figure 1.2 shows the various stages and decisions in the feasibility study.

4 Planning the test

4.1 Site visit

The first step in planning the test will be to visit the site and have a close look at the structure and its surroundings. The access to the structure should be checked together with the access to the parts of the structure where it is proposed to attach instrumentation. It may be necessary to consider providing temporary access to allow the instrumentation and loading equipment to be installed.

During the visit note should be taken of the condition of the structure to check that no serious or significant deterioration has taken place since the previous inspection. It will be necessary to decide what, if any, traffic management measures will be required both for the test itself and for any preparations. For instance, will it be necessary to close the bridge entirely during the test or will it be possible to manage with one-way working controlled by temporary traffic lights? An important consideration will be the time of day when it is proposed to carry out the test as it generally will be easier to obtain complete possession of a carriageway at night.

4.2 Traffic management

The form and extent of the traffic management measures will also be determined to some extent by the method adopted for loading the structure. This will be further complicated if rail possessions or river/canal restrictions are required. On busy roads the traffic management requirements may determine the form of the load test itself, especially if traffic lanes have to be kept open at all times. In extreme cases, the traffic management and the necessity of satisfying, for example, both road and rail requirements may make it impossible to obtain the possessions necessary to carry out any sort of test.

4.3 Loading

The desired positions for the loads to be applied will have been determined as part of the feasibility study. For instance, it will be known whether only global or local loading or a combination of both is to be applied. It will also be known where the loads are to be applied both along and across the structure. These requirements, together with the available possession time, will help to determine the method of loading. In the case of a weak structure it would be advisable to adopt a form of loading which could be released quickly in the event of some unforeseen damage occurring. In considering the possibility of the structure being damaged during the test it is desirable to impose maximum limits on the level of loading that can be applied or the amount of deflection that can be tolerated. Where possession times are restricted it will be necessary to have a method of loading which can be installed and dismantled quickly and which can be easily moved from one location to another.

During the planning process the method of loading and the location of the loading points should be established in sufficient detail for inclusion in a contract specification. If several points are to be loaded simultaneously then co-ordination and control will be an important consideration. There may also be features on the structure itself or in its surrounds which will influence the choice of loading method.

The different methods of loading with their advantages and disadvantages are discussed in Chapter 5.

4.4 Instrumentation

The general location of the instrumentation and the types of measurement required will have been established during the feasibility study. For instance, if the objective is to determine the amount of composite action taking place in a bridge deck it will be necessary to record surface strains across the full depth of the section. The aim of the planning stage should be to establish exactly where on the structure the measurements are to be taken.

An important part of the site inspection will be to confirm or otherwise that the instrumentation can be installed where planned. It may sometimes be necessary to adopt a compromise position if it is not possible to gain access to the desired location. Because of the amount of data that will need to be recorded during a test it will usually be necessary to use data-logging equipment to record loads and responses.

The different techniques and devices available for measuring displacements and strains are discussed in Chapter 6.

4.5 Safety

A crucial consideration in undertaking load testing will be the safety of the travelling public and the personnel involved. The question as to whether or not a structure should be tested will have been answered to some extent in the feasibility study which will have taken account of the condition of the structure and its behaviour under load. Thus, structures which are deemed to be in a bad condition, or where there is a possibility that they could fail in a brittle manner, are likely to have been rejected. However, it is suggested that a risk analysis of the form described in Section 4.6 should always be undertaken before a final decision is made. For vulnerable structures it is essential that the method of loading should be capable of quick removal in the event of an emergency.

The safety of the public must always be paramount. The public will be protected partly by the steps taken to ensure that there is little chance of any damage to the structure. The safety of the bridge users will be one factor in deciding on the appropriate traffic management measures to be imposed both before and during the test. Access under the bridge should not be overlooked and the necessary steps should be taken to safeguard anyone who might have access whether on dry land or on water.

Finally there is an obligation to make sure that all those involved in the testing are kept safe. No one, other than in exceptional circumstances, should be allowed to remain underneath a structure while loads are being applied. Staff should not approach the structure during the application of a load increment until the remote instrumentation has been read and clearance given by the test controller. Protective clothing must be worn by all staff. When the loading is in the form of laden lorries it is important that the drivers are fully briefed and that the bridge is not overloaded by stray vehicles. Where tests are being carried out at night adequate lighting must be provided. Staff must be fully briefed about their duties and responsibilities before the test and only one person must be in overall command with the sole authority to order changes in loading or the abandonment of the test. A comprehensive safety plan should be produced that brings together the health and safety information obtained from the Client, the Engineer who has designed the test and, where appropriate, the planning supervisor in accordance with the Construction (Design and Management) Regulations (1994).

4.6 Risk analysis

There will be a certain element of risk involved in any load test associated with the possibility of damage to the structure and perhaps injury to the public. There will also be certain consequences which must be taken into account if a bridge has to be taken out of service. A form of risk analysis in which the relevant factors can be considered in a formal and structured manner should therefore be undertaken. Since most of the structures being considered for load testing will still be in service and carrying daily traffic they will have shown that they do have some live load-carrying capacity and are not on the point of sudden collapse. Therefore, the perceived risk of anything untoward happening in a well conducted load test is somewhat reduced and such a test can be considered with a reasonable degree of confidence. The main aim of the risk analysis is therefore to ensure that any test is carried out by staff who have appropriate levels of experience and expertise for the risks involved with the particular structure. The form of risk analysis that should be carried out is given in Appendix C. It should be noted that risk analysis of this form still has a considerable subjective element in selecting the factors used.

Two important factors in the risk analysis are the assessment of the susceptibility of the structure and of elements within the structure to brittle-type failures. Examples of such structures and elements are given in Appendix C together with suggested criteria scores. It should be noted that structures with deficient shear capacities at the supports are not suitable for load testing; this includes steel structures which do not have load-bearing stiffeners. Structural elements or details prone to a brittle or buckling-type failure have been given a lower weighting factor than main components because their failure is less likely to lead to a sudden collapse of the complete structure. Such details include internal stiffeners and associated plate panels in plate girders and stiffened plate construction.

4.7 Technical approval

Technical approval procedures should be applied to all supplementary load tests (SLTs) under the direction of the appropriate Technical Approval Authority (TAA). Thus in planning a load test it will be necessary to obtain an approval in principle (AIP) from the TAA for what is proposed. In most cases the supplementary load test is to be carried out within the context of an assessment process which is already under way and subject to the technical approval procedures. In these cases the load test can be regarded as an additional method or criterion the use of which needs to be justified and agreed with the TAA before inclusion in the AIP.

It may be desirable to raise the previously agreed category of the structure if load testing is to be carried out. The decision will depend partly on the perceived risks involved and partly on the extent to which engineering judgement will have to be applied in the interpretation of the results for the long term. Full details of the technical approval procedures for highway structures are given in the *Design Manual for Roads and Bridges* (DMRB 1.1) (1998).

When submitting an application for the inclusion of a load test within an AIP the Engineer should provide the following information:

- the objectives of the load test in terms of the determination and evaluation of any structural actions which are believed to be contributing to the load-carrying capacity of the structure but which cannot be determined by theoretical means
- details of the method of load application including the magnitude and location of the loads and the method of load control
- details of the nature and location of the measurements to be taken and how these will be used in refining the assessment model or in evaluating additional factors contributing to the strength of the structure
- the results of the feasibility study carried out in accordance with Section 3.4
- the results of the risk analysis carried out in accordance with Section 4.6 and proposals for any specialist consultants that are to be employed to carry out the test
- an assessment as to whether the load test is likely to cause any superficial damage to any parts or components of the structure or any services carried by the structure
- the programme for carrying out the load test including the duration of the various activities and any requirements for road closures or possessions
- the precautions to be taken to protect the public and those involved in the load testing.

The AIP should include provision for the checker to certify the potential value, feasibility and safety of a load test following provisional endorsement by the TAA. Full endorsement will follow certification and comments by the checker.

The duties of the checker should include responsibility for ensuring that the feasibility study has been carried out in a diligent manner and the conclusions fully support the proposal for a load test. The checker should also ensure that the results of the load test fully justify any enhancement of the load-carrying capacity of the structure. In particular the checker should carefully scrutinize any enhancements which involve making judgements about long-term effectiveness.

It will not normally be necessary to provide a separate certificate for the load testing since the results will be incorporated in a Certificate F which will include an evaluation of the safe load-carrying capacity of the structure based on the complete assessment process. However, if a serious defect is found during the load test this should be reported to the TAA immediately.

5 Methods of load application

5.1 Introduction

There are many ways in which loading can be applied to a bridge in order to carry out load testing. However, in practice most are too complex and expensive for practical site use and the majority of site load tests have used some form of deadweight system, either kentledge or more usually laden vehicles.

5.2 Review of methods

5.2.1 Dead weights

Dead weights or kentledge blocks can be used to provide distributed or concentrated loads on a bridge deck. A disadvantage is that when placed directly on the surface of the bridge deck as a distributed load, kentledge blocks can in some cases, have a stiffening effect on the structure. Kentledge will require the use of a crane and several vehicles to transport the blocks. The placing of individual blocks is slow and vehicles have to be manoeuvred within range of the crane; removing the load is an equally slow process.

Where kentledge is used for testing small bridges, it can be supported on a frame spanning the structure in a similar manner to a pile test. Concentrated loads can then be applied to the deck by jacking against the dead weight. The applied loads are measured by load cells under the jacks. The advantage of this method is that the load can be quickly removed from the deck by releasing the jack pressure. As an alternative, the supporting frame can be designed to provide the required loading configuration from one of its support reactions. In this case one support is positioned off the bridge whilst the other, which incorporates load cells, is placed at the required loading position. The disadvantage of this method is that the load cannot be quickly removed. In both cases the supports that are not on the bridge will surcharge the abutments and in some types of bridges this may affect the behaviour of the deck.

In all cases where concentrated loads are applied from a loading frame, stability of the loading system should not be overlooked. Test frames are simple to design but often poor geometry can result from the need to load jacks and load cells axially. It is necessary to ensure that the test rig stability will not be compromised when the jacks are fully extended.

5.2.2 Water bags

Flexible water bags can be used to provide dead weight for testing and several different types have been made specially for this use.

(a) Pillow or mattress tanks are either square or rectangular in plan, fully sealed and about 0.5 m high when filled. With some designs it is possible to stack these bags on top of each other, although usually only one additional layer is recommended (see Figure 5.1).

(b) Flexible tanks that work on the flexible dam principle and are open at the top. These tanks can have a circular or rectangular base and can be made up to 100-tonne capacity. The uniform load under the tanks will of course depend on the depth of water and for some designs this can be up to 2.5 m giving a UDL on the structure of 24 kN/m^2 (see Figure 5.2).

(c) Water bags designed to be hung from a structure as a test weight. These bags are mainly used as easily portable test loads for large cranes but they could also be hung beneath bridges to provide concentrated loads at specific points. Their use, however, would be restricted to certain types of bridges where hanging loads could safely provide a realistic alternative to loads applied at deck level. Truss bridges or open deck rail bridges could, for example, be tested using hanging water bags.

Figure 5.1   Pillow tank in use on Westminster Bridge, London.

Figure 5.2   Flexible-dam-type water bag used to simulate floor loading.

The advantages of water bags are that they are easily portable when empty, provide an even distribution of load when placed on the deck and can be filled gradually so that there is no sudden increase in loading. The load applied is measured using a flow meter connected in line with the supply pump. Water bags are ideal where the purpose of the load test is to determine the effect on stresses in particular structural elements, as a result of a large evenly distributed load on the structure. They are especially convenient where the bridge is over a river.

The disadvantages of water bags are that, even with high capacity supply pumps, they can take a long time to fill, and while this is listed as an advantage, it can in some cases be excessive. There also needs to be a large quantity of available water close by where permission can be obtained for pumping and the structure needs to be level to ensure uneven loading does not result (Yeoell et al., 1993). Water bags cannot be unloaded (emptied) as quickly as jacks.

5.2.3 Jacking systems reacting against ground or rock anchors

It is possible to test structures using ground or rock anchor reaction systems and they have been used in conjunction with prestressing jacks and steel test rigs to generate the very large loads required to test bridges to destruction. However, this method is not usually practical for supplementary load testing. It needs favourable conditions at site for anchors to be installed at low cost and requires the design of bridge specific rigs. Reaction systems have the capacity to rapidly generate high loading and safety can be compromised if an error occurs. Because of this, where these systems are used, the testing should only be carried out by specialist consultants and contractors experienced in operating this type of equipment.

5.2.4 HB single-axle trailer

A special single-axle HB test trailer is available for use in load testing (see Figure 5.3). The trailer is arranged so that it can hold specially designed concrete kentledge units symmetrically about the axle. This can provide a single axle loading in increments up to a maximum of 45 tonnes. The trailer also has tubular space frame extensions which can be added to enable the towing vehicle to be clear of the bridge deck. The trailer

Figure 5.3 HB trailer used in loading test on a pipe arch culvert.

Figure 5.4 Loaded lorries in use as a load test.

is an effective means of providing a single heavy axle load but it can only be transported to site in lightly loaded form. It requires additional transport for the kentledge, trailer extensions and the use of a crane for assembly and loading.

5.2.5 Loaded vehicles

Loaded lorries are the most commonly used method of bridge testing (see Figure 5.4). Usually 30–32-tonne four axle rigid aggregate lorries are used as they can be filled to provide the approximate load required and weighed at a weighbridge or on site using portable weigh pads. Different load increments can be provided by using other pre-weighed part loaded vehicles. Due to time constraints additional loading and weighing is often impractical to carry out during load testing, although in some circumstances it may be possible.

It is possible to use strengthened semi-trailers and concrete blocks to provide axle loading incrementally but this requires the use of a small crane to load and redistribute the blocks on the site.

The advantage of vehicle loading is that the load can be easily applied and moved to a variety of positions on the structure. There is no additional equipment on the carriageway other than marks for load positions and therefore the lane can be quickly opened for traffic on completion of the test. It should be noted that where bridge decks are not level or have poor surfacing, wheel loads may be uneven and would be best measured at the load position using portable weigh pads. However, this would take too long to be practical for other than a small number of load positions.

5.3 Railway loading

When testing rail under-bridges, locomotives can be used as static or moving loads. It is difficult to weigh rail vehicles as rail weighbridges are not common on the system. This is not necessarily a problem however, as the variability of locomotive axle weights is low. In tests where the wheel loads are critical, portable calibrated wheel jacks can be used to weigh the locomotive on site.

The use of rail traffic loading on rail under-bridges is popular with rail engineers, and because of the excitation that can be caused by a long train, measurements of the natural frequency and damping are important. The weights of locomotives, particularly electric locomotives, are reliably known and the weights of certain trains, i.e. those comprised of 100-tonne loaded aggregate waggons, will also be fairly predictable. There is a rail weigh-in-motion system available that uses a rail shear bridge, essentially a strain-gauged rail, to measure vertical load. This equipment has however, been mainly used in research for statistical studies of rail vehicle loads.

The speed of trains during dynamic testing can be determined easily using a radar gun or, as the length of the train is usually known, it can simply be timed passing a particular location. The latter method is usually preferred as it is safer for the testing staff and less alarming for the train drivers.

6 Measuring equipment

6.1 Introduction

The correct type, amount and location of instrumentation used on a structure during a load test is critical to achieving a satisfactory outcome. Instrumentation is labour intensive to install, and while too much instrumentation can be a waste of resources, too little can seriously compromise a test. The design of suitable instrumentation schemes needs experience and a good appreciation of the likely structural behaviour of a bridge. The suitability of the instrumentation for the expected measurement range requires careful consideration. Small deflection measurements for example could be swamped by temperature effects.

In the context of supplementary load testing the objective is often to quantify an effect which is known to exist and could be beneficial to the assessment. In this case the instrumentation required can be targeted and may be relatively simple.

6.2 Displacements

When supplementary load testing is carried out the instrumentation specified must be capable of resolving small displacements.

For deflections the transducers most commonly used are either potentiometric (geared rotary or linear potentiometers), linear variable displacement transformers (LVDT) and in some cases manually read dial gauges. These can be mounted on some form of independent stand or scaffold and either bear directly on the structure or be attached vertically below it using invar wires. Invar wires are used to minimize the effect of temperature change and should be kept short and tensioned to prevent wind induced oscillation (see Figure 6.1).

In the rail industry a system has been developed that allows deflections to be rapidly obtained at low cost using specially designed telescopic poles (Packham, 1993). The poles are erected pneumatically and utilize a 50-mm stroke spring-loaded transducer pre-compressed to 25 mm against the soffit of the bridge. Three poles are used to obtain true deflection with reference to the bearings. The poles are used mainly under normal rail traffic loading and data are logged to a dedicated ruggedized waterproofed data logger with a display screen allowing the deflection history for each pole to be viewed. The logger scans the poles at 100 Hz which is sufficient to capture high-frequency deflection changes under high-speed rail traffic. The system is used for supplementary testing to determine the behaviour of bridge decks for assessment and also for routine monitoring purposes. There is also a mobile strain gauge (MST) system which can utilize the same logging system as the deflection poles.

Figure 6.1 *Bridge soffit showing vibrating strain gauges and LVDT dislacement transducer.*

There are other ways of measuring displacements such as electro-levels, laser techniques and photogrammetry. Some are more effective than others and some will be capable of further development in the future. Laser theodolite systems, when sited on a target attached to the structure, can be used to determine deflections under rapidly moving loads. However, these systems can suffer from atmospheric distortion over long distances as would any optical system. A system has been used successfully by researchers in the rail industry to monitor deflections on bridges. It is able, in good atmospheric conditions, to resolve displacement to better than 0.5 mm in both the vertical and horizontal directions under rapidly moving loads. It is, however, complicated and expensive to calibrate. Photogrammetric methods are routinely used to check rail tunnels for displacement and a scanning displacement system of greater accuracy could be useful for comparative tests on masonry arch bridges. A suitable system could be used similarly to the deflection pole equipment used for rail bridges, but provide much more extensive information.

6.3 Strains

The instruments used for measuring strain in situ are chosen with regard to the type of material, gauge length, space available for mounting and whether the measurements are to be static or dynamic. Vibrating wire gauges and demec gauges can be used on concrete and steel structures. Electrical resistance strain gauges (ERS) are more readily adopted for metal structures though some require considerable surface preparation. Special types are occasionally used on concrete where dynamic measurements are required.

6.3.1 Vibrating wire gauges

Vibrating wire (VW) gauges comprise a fine wire tensioned between mounting blocks and protected by a metal tube. The wire is energized by a coil which also serves to read the frequency at which it then vibrates. The coil can be an integral or detachable part of the gauge and can also incorporate a thermistor or utilize coil resistance for temperature measurement. For a 140 mm gauge length the resolution attainable is 0.5 micro strain over a range of 3000 micro strain. The gauges can be designed for surface mounting, for embedment in concrete or for crack monitoring and they are long lasting and stable. Surface-mounted gauges can be installed with little surface preparation using epoxy- or polyester-based glues and in many instances can be recovered after the test.

VW gauges have the advantage that they read frequency and therefore are not affected by slight changes in the electrical resistance of the circuit. Therefore they do not have to be hard wired or have particularly high-quality connectors to work effectively. The gauges can be read directly using a simple robust measuring unit or by a dedicated multi-channel logger with digital output to a computer or other storage device.

The disadvantage of standard VW gauges is that they can only be read discretely. This is not a problem where strains due to static loads are being measured but it prevents their use for dynamic tests. Continuously vibrating wire gauges have been produced for dynamic strain measurement but these have not been widely used.

6.3.2 Demec gauges

Hand-held demec (demountable mechanical) gauges have been used routinely in testing in the past and can be effective in certain circumstances. Pre-drilled studs are fixed to the structure using epoxy adhesive and a calibration bar. The measuring instrument comprises a spring loaded lever system operating a dial gauge. Pins protruding from the instrument are located in the studs and the dial gauge read manually. The equipment is available in a range of gauge lengths although 100 mm, 200 mm and 250 mm are the most common. With care the instrument can be read to an accuracy of 2.5 µm (10 micro strain for gauge length of 250 mm). Again the temperature of the structure is important and corrections should be made by comparison with an invar bar at a known temperature.

The equipment is robust and relatively simple and cheap to use. It is particularly suitable for simple tests where there are small numbers of gauge positions close together at one point on the structure. The manual operation is, however, time consuming and demec gauges are better suited to long-term monitoring.

6.3.3 Electrical resistance strain gauges

Electrical resistance strain (ERS) gauges are normally used on metal structures. They comprise a fine grid of wires etched from copper/nickel foil. They can be produced to a variety of sizes and configurations, including rosettes of multiple gauges, to determine principal stresses. They are of high accuracy, can be read continuously and therefore can be used for dynamic measurement. ERS gauges require considerable surface preparation and the services of a trained technician for installation. They are either bonded or spot welded to a prepared surface depending on the type of gauge. Weldable gauges tend to be used in long-term applications or more difficult environments. Because ERS gauges measure electrical resistance they need to be hard-wired or have high-quality connectors to reliably connect to a data logger. Some demountable electrical resistance gauges have been developed which use ERS gauges instead of a dial gauge as in the demec gauge described above. These gauges are able to be clamped to part of the structure and logged over time. They can be useful for investigating the level of strain at different locations in the structure under normal traffic loading, prior to deciding the position of instrumentation for a load test.

6.4 Temperature

The main method of determining bridge deck temperature is by means of thermocouples. Thermocouples for ambient temperature measurement are made using special two core copper/constantan cable and rely on the junction of dissimilar metals causing a current to flow that is dependant on temperature. This is known as the 'Seebeck' effect. Two junctions are made, one is where the temperature is to be measured and the other, reference junction, is at a lower temperature. The temperature difference between the junctions causes an electromagnetic force and flow of current. In practice loggers for thermocouples simulate the reference junction electronically. Thermocouples can be installed in the bridge or on the surface of the material. Some strain gauge systems (see VW gauges above) also integrate temperature measurements into the gauge.

The measurement of temperature is very important during testing. Temperature changes during the course of a test can significantly affect the strains in the bridge deck. If at all possible, the instrumentation should be monitored prior to the test to determine the effects of temperature change on the deck.

A summary of the instrumentation transducers and systems is given in Table 6.1.

6.5 Data recording

6.5.1 Data loggers

Before considering data loggers it is important to note that any mains electricity-powered electronic equipment operated at site for data collection purposes will require a stabilized and non-interruptible power supply. Without this equipment there is a risk of data loss, as generators suitable for running small tools, etc. can be unreliable sources for powering loggers and computers.

Table 6.1   Summary of instrumentation transducers and systems

Instrumentation systems	Principal applications	Suitable load conditions	Suitable structures	Types of equipment	Remarks
LVDT	Displacement	Static, dynamic	No restriction	Electrical	Rigid mounting required
Deflection pole	Displacement	Static, dynamic	No restriction	Electrical	Quick to set up, very efficient data recording
Dial gauge	Displacement	Static	No restriction	Mechanical	Manual reading and rigid mounting required
Laser theodolite systems	Displacement related	Static, dynamic	No restriction	Laser	Good for two-dimensional displacement
Vibrating wire VW gauge	Strain	Static	No restriction	Acoustic	Easy to glue to any surface, accurate, can be temperature sensing
Electrical resistance strain ERS gauge	Strain	Static, dynamic	Metal, concrete	Electrical	Accurate and reliable but costly, requires special skills
Demountable ERS gauge	Strain	Static, dynamic	Masonry, metal, timber	Electrical	Accurate and reliable but not widely used
Mobile strain transducer	Strain	Static, dynamic	Metal	Electrical	Used in conjunction with deflection pole system
Demec gauge	Strain	Static	No restriction	Mechanical	Easy to use but human error can be significant
Accelerometers	Vibration	Dynamic	No restriction	Electrical	Accurate if used correctly
Thermocouples	Temperature	Static, dynamic	No restriction	Electrical	Easy to make and use on site

There are many different forms of data logger available; most can operate in stand-alone form or in conjunction with a personal computer. The advantage of a system linked to a computer is that it enables monitoring and analysis to be carried out on site, and immediate plots of output from the instrumentation.

The main requirements of data-logging equipment for site are that it should be robust, capable of logging the required number of channels and have adequate backup facilities. In practice back up facilities are often provided via the linked computer and should include a hard copy plus disk, tape or optical drive. There should be no question of data being lost and a hard copy should be produced at the time to provide the final assurance.

It should be noted that vibrating wire strain gauges require a logging system capable of energizing the gauge and reading frequency. Loggers such as these are therefore usually supplied by the manufacturers of the gauges.

The need to provide accommodation, cabling and a suitable power supply for a data logging system means that for many tests on small structures it may be more cost effective and simpler to log instrumentation manually with hand-held equipment. A combination of data logger and manual logging can also be used where appropriate to simplify the system. In each case a clear means of identifying data with load position or increment is important in order to cross reference data correctly.

6.5.2 Video recording and photography

The use of a video record during a test is recommended. Video recording is cheap and can give a continuous record of the procedure during the test. If any anomaly is subsequently found, for example a gross error in load position, this is likely to be identified from the video. The video will also allow a record of any practical problems found and the time taken for each operation to be recorded for future reference.

During the test the use of photography is important for recording instrumentation layouts, load positions, existing defects in the structure and the condition of bridge components, etc. Photographs can be useful during the analysis in identifying why results from the instrumentation may not be consistent and can highlight the differing condition of components, ingress of water, quality of concrete, etc. They are essential for illustrating the test report. Where the bridge is only partially closed during testing video and photography can provide a record of the traffic levels on the areas of the deck that are still open.

7   Test procedures

7.1   Introduction

This chapter covers the test procedures for a complex test. In many cases however, tests can be carried out with minimum traffic disruption and simple instrumentation. Where this is the case much of what is listed below may not apply.

7.2   Initial planning

A load test is a short duration specialized activity usually carried out under some form of road closure. It therefore requires meticulous planning if it is not to be compromised by any unforseen delays.

7.2.1   Test plan and staffing requirements

A detailed test plan is necessary to ensure that all those involved have a full understanding of what is required and the time constraints on each activity. The test plan is also important, if there is any delay during testing, to enable decisions on the remedial action necessary to finish to programme.

A typical test plan should include the following:

- road closure/possession times
- a Gantt chart showing the different activities, their planned duration and float times
- positioning of loads
- positioning of instrumentation
- details of the instrumentation used for each load position (where different)
- data security arrangements (hard copy, disk, tape, optical)
- schedule of staff required and duties
- plant and equipment schedule
- risk assessment and safety plan
- emergency procedures
- emergency telephone numbers.

The numbers of staff required to carry out the test will depend on its size, complexity, the amount of instrumentation and the number of tasks that have to be carried out concurrently. They comprise:

- Team leader in overall charge of the test who should be a chartered engineer with experience of bridge testing.
- Engineer/technician for logging data, on site interpretation of data and comparison with calculated responses.
- Electrician.
- Staff for directing and positioning loads, survey duties and controlling load intensity where this is variable.

- Vehicle drivers and plant operatives.
- Staff to closely monitor the structure and any existing defects during load application.
- Staff as required to assist with directing members of the public.

7.2.2 Liaison with other bodies

The police, ambulance and fire services will be informed where there is to be a road closure in operation. However, because instrumentation and cabling has in the past been mistaken for evidence of terrorist activity, the police in particular need to be informed about the type of work being carried out.

For bridges over rivers and canals the appropriate authority will need to be consulted regarding any restriction of the navigation or water course, and also to ensure no pollution occurs. These could be the Environment Agency, relevant port authority or the British Waterways Board. Where water bags are used for loading, permission will have to be obtained for pumping. Some activities carried out by the authorities could affect testing at certain times of the year. Weed cutting, for example, can result in damage or movement of scaffolding where it is standing in the river and the release of sluices, locks and weirs can rapidly change water levels.

The locations of utilities need to be known and checked so that no damage can be caused to them.

Where bridges are over railways, track possessions will have to be applied for well in advance of the test date. The times quoted may well be total possession time between trains and not include time taken to switch off the traction current and notify the site that it is safe to work. This can vary according to local conditions and it is important to obtain a reliable estimate of available working time from the rail infrastructure owner. Where instrumentation is in place and trains are running prior to the test it may be affected by the proximity of any high voltage equipment. Stray currents can be induced where electric traction is in operation. As with the police, the rail infrastructure owner will need to be informed of the details of the instrumentation so that it is not mistaken for evidence of terrorist activity. Tests on railway bridges may, at the discretion of the infrastructure owner, require the preparation of a safety case for submission to the relevant safety assessment panel. This document can be substantial as it must address all possible areas of risk in the preparation and conduct of the test.

Liaison with the local authority (often the client) will be required to arrange a date and time for the test and the necessary road closures. The local authority can often also help in identifying a suitable site close by for parking vehicles and safe storage of equipment.

In general, the bridge owner needs to be made fully aware of what is proposed, including any tests or installation that may cause damage. Surface preparation for gauges for example may compromise the paint system and require subsequent repairs. Excavation of a small amount of surfacing may be needed to instrument at the deck surface and obtain a strain profile. In all cases there is a need to obtain the client's specification for the type of repairs that may be required.

7.2.3 Date and time of test

Load testing is often carried out at night when there is less traffic and bridge deck temperatures are most stable. This is particularly important for supplementary testing where the effects of loading could be swamped by the effects of temperature change.

The time of year that the test is carried out will also have an effect. For example, where ambient temperatures are high, surfacing stiffness will be low and the converse will be the case when ambient temperatures are low. Where composite action with the deck is likely to occur, surfacing stiffness could have a significant effect. Instrumentation would have to be arranged to detect and quantify this, whether or not it is invoked in the subsequent assessment.

7.3 Site preparation

The amount of site preparation that can be done prior to the test will depend on local conditions. In the worst case, access both above and below the bridge will be limited and additional pre-test closures under the bridge will be necessary for the installation of instrumentation.

Where access below the bridge requires scaffolding, this can often be designed to double as support for displacement transducers providing it is independent of the structure.

A survey of the structure will have to be carried out to position instrumentation and loading points. Suitable setting out stations however can be established off the carriageway to enable the load positions to be set out simply during the test. Once everything is prepared any installation that could not be positioned as planned will have to be resurveyed and its revised location noted. Where possible the loading positions should be clearly identified and numbered using marking paint.

7.4 Installation of instruments

The correct setting up of the instrumentation is vital for the success of a test. It is important to be aware of what is being measured and how certain effects, movements or failures, could compromise that measurement. Electrical faults on the site can take time to trace and therefore all cabling and equipment should be thoroughly tested beforehand.

7.4.1 Transducers

When installing transducers for the measurement of displacement the main requirement is for a rigid support. This can be in the form of a tubular scaffold with transducers fixed to special scaffold clips or specially designed stands. Transducers are also required at the abutments to ensure that the displacements measured elsewhere in the span are not the result of bearing movement. Where there is confidence in the integrity of the abutments the transducers can be located on the bearing shelves using weighted stands otherwise they need to be fixed to an independent support.

Transducers that are spring loaded and work in compression need to bear on a smooth, level part of the structure. In the event of this not being available small steel wedges cut at the appropriate angle can be glued to the structure to provide a level surface.

Transducers that work in tension will need to be attached to the structure using invar wire. These wires should be kept short so that they are not affected by air movement. Attachment to the structure is usually by means of hooks fixed to small plates which are glued in place. Most transducers will have sufficient range of movement for supplementary testing; however it is important when installing them to ensure they are correctly positioned so that their range is not exceeded during the test. It is also sensible to have a simple portable apparatus with a fixed test dimension between two points so that any transducer can be checked for accuracy on site.

7.4.2 Strain gauges

The installation of electrical resistance strain gauges is a specialized process requiring careful surface preparation and fixing by a trained technician. The gauges are either glued in place using cyano-acrylate ('Superglue') or welded using specialist micro-spot-welding equipment. As described in Section 6.3.3, ERS gauges need to have good-quality connectors or be hard-wired.

Vibrating wire gauges are simpler and can, with some tuition and practice, be installed by most site staff. In most cases VW gauges can be glued to the structure using a filled polyester adhesive, usually the non-elastic form of that used for car-body repairs. This adhesive will not fix to wet surfaces and cold temperatures result in greatly extended setting times. The adhesive is adequate to attach gauges to a rough surface but is not so strong that they cannot be recovered afterwards. Some specialists use industrial adhesives or dental cement which can overcome the disadvantages detailed above, but these can be expensive and are often only available in larger quantities. Vibrating wire gauges can also be fixed using screw fixings but some damage to the structure will be caused by drilling.

To install the gauges, they are first set by adjusting the spacing tube so that the wires are tensioned to vibrate at the required frequency. The frequency setting depends on whether the strain during the test is expected to be positive or negative. If this is not known gauges are set to the centre of their usable range. They are then glued in place on the structure. When the adhesive has cured, the spacing tube is slackened off so that the wire is then held between the two fixed mounting blocks. Its frequency of vibration will then correlate with change of strain over the gauge length.

Unless it is intended to monitor crack movement it is important, when installing VW gauges on concrete, to ensure that there are no existing surface cracks near the gauge. A crack through the gauge will measure a large increase in strain if it opens during testing whereas a crack near but outside the gauge length may have the opposite effect. Similarly a gauge placed on a previous concrete repair may also not record the true strain at that point.

Once in place VW gauges can be cabled back to a multi-channel logger or read discretely using a portable strain measuring unit.

7.5 Load application

Whatever form of loading is chosen it is important to ensure that it does not exceed the maximum planned loading obtained from the pre-test analysis. Using pre-weighed vehicles, this can be largely assured. Other kentledge systems can also be similarly restricted by simple controls on site. Hydraulic jacking systems however, need more care because, in the event of an error, a considerable overload can be quickly developed.

Where loads are applied using pre-weighed vehicles, the exact positions of the loads are important and they will require positioning both laterally and longitudinally at pre-marked locations. Adequate time for this needs to be allowed in the programme, especially if a number of loading positions are required.

Load application using other forms of dead weight such as kentledge and waterbags will be incremental, allowing data to be logged on an incremental basis while load is being applied and removed.

In tests where multi-point loads are applied either by jacking against kentledge or ground anchors there needs to be some method of load balancing, otherwise one jack can have the effect of relieving the others. Whether load balancing is a problem large-ly depends on the load positions and the design of the test rig. Where the required loads are equal and jacks are identical they can, in theory, be linked hydraulically at the same pressure. But in practice seal friction would vary and result in some unequal loading. It is usually better to use separately controlled jacks bearing on load cells. Generally to read load reliably from jack pressure requires specially designed low friction jacks which are not normally available.

7.6 Measuring responses

The instrumentation should be logged several times for the zero load case, preferably for some time before the test commences, so that any trends in temperature response are identified. For each load position or increment the instrumentation should be logged immediately after load application and immediately before the next position or increment. Experienced testing engineers will habitually log several scans of data between increments, though this may not be practical where data are recorded manually.

Where load is being incremented it is recommended that a load/maximum displace-ment plot is displayed and updated continuously to give an early indication of any non-linear response.

The structure should be observed carefully at each load position or increment with any significant observations relayed to the test controller. In particular, existing defects should be monitored closely for any changes that may be significant. Staff log-ging the instrumentation will be given strain and displacement limits established from the pre-test analysis. They will regularly scan the data being recorded to ensure no sensor is recording any excessive changes or approaching these limits. If this happens the test should be halted and the cause established before proceeding. The occurrence of non-linear behaviour should be reported immediately.

The temperature will be recorded but any changes in weather conditions should be noted, together with the time at which they occurred. Sudden rain can cause a rapid cooling of the deck and sensors, and high wind can cause detectable movement in sensors and support structures. After completion of the test, when loading is removed, gauges should be read to check that they return to zero and there is no permanent deflection of the structure.

7.7 Emergency procedures

Other than on the smallest sites radio communication between staff is central to any emergency procedures. If any problem is noticed the test can be halted immediately and the loading removed. It should be noted that vehicle loading and hydraulic load-ing can be removed rapidly but kentledge and water ballast cannot.

All staff should be in possession of the emergency procedures and emergency service contact numbers contained within the test plan. A briefing on the emergency procedures should be carried out before the test commences. In all cases the emergency services will be aware of the work from previous contact (see Section 7.2.2).

7.8 Clearance of site

On completion of the testing the site should be cleared. This will entail removing any equipment and plant from the vicinity of the bridge deck, spraying out any load posi-tioning paint marks and making good any damage to the surfacing. Beneath the bridge the instrumentation and cabling should be removed and any resulting damage to the paint system or concrete surface repaired in accordance with the client's requirements (see Section 7.2.2).

On completion of the work, and after a general site inspection by the test controller to ensure the site is clear and safe, the road can be re-opened to the public.

8   Interpretation of results

8.1   Introduction

This chapter deals with the use of the load test results for calculating an improved value of the safe load-carrying capacity of the structure. Generally, the results will consist of measured strains and/or displacements which are associated with loading configurations and intensities. It is important to remember that it is the physical behaviour of the structure which is important rather than the fact that it has endured a certain level of loading.

At least one method of analysis should be undertaken and a mathematical model of the structure set up which can be modified in the light of the test results. This analysis should be sufficiently powerful to provide a good indication of how the structure would behave when load tested. It is not expected that a completely new mathematical idealization of the structure will be necessary unless the test has revealed an unexpected response.

8.2   Comparison of measured and calculated results

The main aim of the supplementary load test is to improve the analytical modelling of the structure. Thus the first action is to compare the calculated responses of the structure with those measured under the test loading. The comparison should not only be done in absolute terms but also qualitatively to see, for instance, if the transverse deflection profiles have a similar shape. In most cases it will be found that the measured responses are significantly lower than the calculated ones.

8.2.1   Linearity

One thing to establish is whether the structure is behaving in a linear manner, where changes in loading produce corresponding pro-rata changes in deflections and strains which return to zero when load is removed. Evidence of non-linear behaviour might be an indication of some serious fault in the structure and should be investigated further. At the lower levels of loading the measured responses may be very small and could be distorted by experimental errors in the measuring equipment. Thus, before any results are used for comparative purposes they need to be carefully scrutinized for consistency with any unexplained anomalies or obvious erroneous values being discarded.

8.2.2   Dead weight

It should be remembered that the structure will already be carrying its own self-weight together with the superimposed dead weight from surfacing and non-structural components. An important part of the assessment process will be to determine what proportion of the load-carrying capacity of the structure is required to carry these loads. The effect of the dead loading on the structure depends to some extent on the method and sequence of construction and information about this can be obtained from site records and as-built drawings. In many cases, because of the evenly distributed nature of dead loading, its effects can be accurately determined without recourse to load distribution methods of analysis. However, in other cases, such as in the ribs of a cast-iron arch, the dead load stresses may be difficult to determine analytically and it will be necessary to find them experimentally using one of the techniques described in Appendix B.

8.2.3 Stiffness

An evaluation of the test results should indicate whether, and in what way, the structure is stiffer than assumed in the calculations. Generally lower deflections all over the structure could indicate that the calculated longitudinal stiffness parameters are too low; a flatter transverse deflection profile could be an indication that the calculated transverse stiffness parameters are too low. Some of these effects could also arise from other factors such as rotational restraint at the supports, produced by the surfacing over the joint, or seized bearings. An inspection of the longitudinal deflection profile together with any strain measurements taken near the supports could indicate whether there is some form of boundary restraint. The stiffness of the structure can also be affected by non-structural components such as parapets which, in practice, act with the structure and contribute to its load-carrying capacity.

8.2.4 Local effects

The discussions so far have concerned the behaviour of the structure acting as a complete body. However, in some cases the apparent shortfall in load capacity is determined by the capacity of an element or component under a local load. In these cases there may be a slightly different approach to the way in which the results of the load test are used, since the objective of the test may have been to confirm whether or not some other structural action, apart from bending and shear, is taking place. For instance where a concentrated load is applied to the concrete deck of a beam and slab type bridge, the development of in-plane compressive membrane stresses can contribute to the load resistance of the slab, which can carry greater loads than would be calculated from bending and punching shear calculations alone. Thus a study of the measured surface strains in the vicinity of the applied load could indicate whether membrane action is being mobilized and can be taken into account in the assessment. Such a decision would be based on a scrutiny of the measured strains by themselves with no reference to any calculated values.

8.3 Calibration of structural models

As discussed the comparison of the calculated and measured deformations should indicate whether adjustments are needed in the input to the analytical model of the structure. The next stage will be an iterative one in which the structure is re-analysed using adjusted input parameters until an optimum solution is found where the calculated and measured values match as closely as possible. The adjustments to the input data need to be undertaken in a logical and methodical manner so that it is possible to distinguish the effects of the various changes from each other. For instance if it is felt that the assumed transverse stiffness properties are incorrect it would be better to adjust these separately from adjusting, say, the longitudinal stiffnesses although in many analysis programs it is the ratio of longitudinal to transverse stiffness which is important rather than the absolute values of either. Since in most cases some form of linear elastic analysis will be used it should be fairly easy to establish a relationship between changes in a particular input parameter and the corresponding changes in the output values and so arrive fairly quickly at the optimum idealization of the structure.

It is unlikely that it will be possible to achieve a good match between every measured and calculated value even with the modified analytical model and so it will be necessary to decide which of the values are most important to match. For instance, it may be thought more important to match the profiles of the transverse deflection rather than the absolute deflection values. The optimum solution adopted may also depend upon the nature of the load capacity shortfall; for example in the case of a bending resistance deficiency, more weight would be given to achieving a match between longitudinal deflections than to other measurements.

As already mentioned in the case of local deficiencies it may not always be necessary to revise the analytical model. The results from the load test itself could well be sufficient to confirm whether the suspected form of structural action is being mobilized and is providing additional resistance to the local load. The measured results would give confidence that this additional factor could be taken into account in the calculations with its contribution being determined by reference to codes of practice or research findings.

8.4 Estimation of load capacity

8.4.1 Ultimate limit state

It would be ideal if the safe load capacity of a structure could be deduced directly from load tests carried out in the elastic range. However this would require knowledge of the behaviour of individual elements over the whole elastic–plastic range and of the way that loads were shared between adjacent elements as the complete structure neared collapse. Although there are some particular types of element for which it is possible to predict collapse behaviour from behaviour in the elastic range when tested in isolation, such examples are few. In any case in a real structure the elements are interconnected and their behaviour is influenced by the end restraints provided by the adjacent elements. It is this relatively complex and unique nature of most bridge structures that makes it impossible to derive a safe load capacity directly from load tests in the elastic range with any degree of confidence. The most effective role of supplementary load testing is in providing a better understanding of the global and local behaviour of a particular structure and hence in improving the analytical model so that it more closely mirrors that of the real structure. It follows therefore that some form of analysis must be carried out before undertaking any load test.

Once the analytical model has been calibrated against the test results, as described in Section 8.3, the optimized model can be used to re-analyse the structure at the ultimate limit state or ULS (except for cast iron and masonry structures which are assessed by different principles). This re-analysis and subsequent checking against the appropriate codes will show whether the structure may be deemed capable of carrying the required loading in full. Hopefully there should have been some improvement in load-carrying capacity over the previous calculations, but where this is still inadequate it will be necessary to adopt one of the measures discussed in Section 2.8. It will be noted that any predictions for the ultimate limit state are done within the analytical process itself with factored element strengths being checked against the factored loading effects obtained using the revised analytical model.

8.4.2 Reliability

A difficulty with supplementary load testing is to determine how far any improvement in the analytical model, which has been determined by testing at fairly low levels of loading, can be assumed to be still effective at the ultimate limit state. This concerns both the basic mechanism of transverse load distribution and enhancements due to factors such as uncertain composite action which would not normally be considered in a theoretical assessment. These two distinct problem areas concerning the reliability of the load test findings at higher levels of loading are discussed below; the long-term reliability of load test findings are discussed in Section 8.5.

8.4.3 Load distribution

In cases where the transverse distribution is affected by a form of construction which is not amenable to analysis, such as masonry jack arches, it may be necessary to refer to published reports of collapse tests on similar structures. If the transverse medium remained intact throughout the test then it would be reasonable to assume that the transverse distribution characteristics had not changed significantly as the load was increased. In cases where the distribution is affected by more conventional construction details, which are amenable to analysis, it is reasonable to assume that the assumptions made in design about the constancy of structural behaviour throughout the loading range also hold good for assessment.

Some research has shown that the transverse distribution mechanisms determined from supplementary load testing do remain effective right up to the point of collapse (Cullington and Beales, 1995). In the case of a bridge deck with longitudinal beams and masonry jack arches, it was found that the jack arches remained intact and effective up unitil the collapse of the structure. In another case it was found that although the structure remained intact until collapse, the behaviour of the structure at collapse was best represented by a somewhat different model from that which had been assumed initially. Here a filler beam deck was found to be acting as though there were raking struts between the individual beams and that the deck could be assessed as a 'shear key' deck using elastic load distribution methods.

8.4.4 Additional strength factors

The other assumption that needs to be examined is whether the other effects which enhance the perceived load-carrying capacity of a structure also remain effective at the higher loading levels. The individual contributions of end restraint or composite action are difficult to extract from load test results and it is difficult to determine how far effects such as these remain effective as loads and strains are increased. The decision whether or not to rely on the contribution of a certain factor will depend on a number of things. If the shortfall in capacity without the additional factor is marginal and the effect of the additional factor is more than sufficient to pass the structure then it may be felt that, despite any uncertainty about its long-term effectiveness, it will be safe to consider the structure as being up to standard. Again if the measured strains and deflections are much lower than calculated, even with an adjusted analytical model, it may well be felt that even with doubts over the reliability of the additional factor its contribution can be relied on because of the mobilization of other unidentified sources of strength. However in some cases it may be sensible to consider a reduction in the contribution from these types of effect at the ultimate state. Here again reference to published collapse tests may help the engineer to decide whether the contribution from a certain factor is still likely to be as effective at higher levels of loading.

8.4.5 Collapse tests

Care must be taken when applying the results of collapse tests on other structures to the structure under investigation. The engineer will have to decide whether the reported behaviour is truly relevant and described in sufficient detail. Some engineers may take the view that a one-off collapse test cannot be treated as being necessarily representative of all bridges of that type. On the other hand others may consider that the results can be transferred with some confidence and that the additional structural actions which have been identified can be relied on at loads higher than those applied in the supplementary tests. Details of published collapse tests which may be relevant and which can provide assurance or otherwise of the reliability of structural actions up to collapse and the mechanisms of collapse are given in Table 8.1.

8.4.6 Retrofixing

One way of ensuring that the source of additional strength remains effective at higher load levels is by modifying the structure to provide the physical mechanism to bring this action into effect. It is not strengthening in the conventional sense, neither should it be regarded as maintenance or refurbishment. An example would be the provision of some form of physical connection between the steel members of a trough deck and the concrete infill to ensure that the composite action mobilized at the lower loads through friction did not become disconnected at higher loads.

8.4.7 Recommended method

A number of questions have been raised about the derivation of the safe load-carrying capacity of a structure from the results of supplementary load tests. In order that the various questions can be addressed in a logical and consistent manner it is recommended that the method outlined in Figure 8.1 should be followed. The methodology is to be used after the supplementary load test data are assessed and the structural re-analysis carried out. It is based on a series of questions:

- Is there evidence of additional strength?
- Are relevant collapse data available?
- Can a mechanism of extra strength be identified from structural analysis?
- Can a mechanism of extra strength be identified from published collapse data?
- Is the mechanism of extra strength reliable up to ULS?
- If unreliable, can it be retrofixed?
- If unreliable, will it be appropriate to monitor the structure?
- If unreliable, will it be appropriate to carry out periodic SLTs?

The term 'additional strength' encompasses the enhanced load-carrying capacity available both from the mobilization of certain structural actions as well as that derived from better load distribution. The evidence for additional strength will be available from knowledge of the behaviour of similar structures as well as from observations of the structure in question, which may well be carrying greater loads than predicted by calculation with no signs of distress. The careful location of the instrumentation attached to the structure should enable different mechanisms of extra strength to be identified. The 'reliability' of the mechanisms providing the extra strength refers to the likelihood or otherwise of the sources of that strength becoming disconnected both at higher loading and with time.

8.4.8 Safety margins

It is important to note that in assessing the load-carrying capacity of a structure, it is not just a question of demonstrating that the structure can carry specified maximum traffic loads but that it can do so with adequate margins of safety. Although the normal analytical process may be conservative, in that it is concerned with the strength of individual elements rather than the strength of the structure behaving as a complete entity, it does allow an appropriate predetermined margin of safety to be incorporated. It is very difficult to determine from the results of a load test alone what margins of safety might be available in the structure, unless the structure happens to be a fairly simple one from a family whose load/displacement behaviour up to collapse is fully understood and is repeatable. Most real life structures do not fall into this category and there is always the danger that a structure which can apparently support a given load without distress may collapse suddenly with a small increase in the load.

Table 8.1 Details of collapse tests

Type of bridge	Comments on performance	Failure load (kN)	Reference
Filler beam	Four-point loading, ductile bending	2900	Low, A. McC. and Ricketts, N. TRL report RR 383
Reinforced concrete beam and slab (components in-situ)			Ricketts, N.J. and Low, A. McC. TRL report RR 377
slab	Hennebique construction, point loading applied to each component. Punch through failure.	2900	
cross beam	Combined shear and slab punch failure.	2750	
main beam 1 (poor condition)	Large flexural cracks but unable to fail.	5250	
main beam 2 (good condition)	Large flexural cracks but unable to fail.	5200	
Masonry arches	Line loading		Page, J
Preston	Arch ring crushing. Poor condition, no parapets, distorted arch, four hinge failure. Three-hinge snap through failure.	2110	TRL report RR 110
Prestwood		228	TRL report RR 110
Torksey	Four-hinge failure. Rubble masonry, poor condition. 29° skew, ashlar masonry, good condition. Load tests to failure of 11 arch bridges between 1984 and 1994.	1080	TRL report RR 159
Shinafoot		2524	TRL report RR 159
Strathmashie		1325	TRL report RR 201
Barlae		2900	TRL Report RR 201. Melbourne, C. and
Load tests to collapse on masonry arch bridges			Page, J. *Proceedings of the First Conference on Arch Bridges*, 1995
General			
Various	Tests described for hogging plate, two jack arches and trough deck		Cullington, D.W. and Beales, C. (1994). *ICE Bridge Modification Conference*

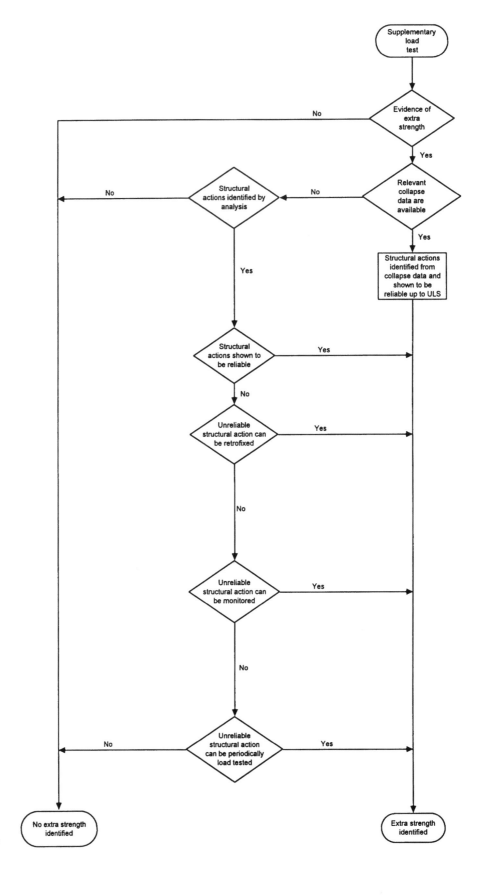

Figure 8.1   Flowchart for the interpretation of supplementary load test data.

This disadvantage of load testing is overcome when load testing is used as a means of improving the assessment procedures rather than as an end in itself. Supplementary load testing alone cannot determine the reserve of strength in the structure.

8.5 Long-term reliability

Bridges are long-life structures and full account must be taken of the long-term reliability of any factors which have been used in revising the load-bearing capacity of the structure.

8.5.1 Composite action

If composite action is found to be taking place between the concrete infill and the supporting steel trough with no shear connectors it is important to consider whether this composite action can be relied on for the remaining life of the structure. The composite action could be lost if the structure were accidentally overloaded or even if it were subjected to legal loads which were substantially higher than experienced in the past. The reliability of some of these contributing factors can be affected by temperature such as in the case of asphalt surfacing where the additional stiffness it provides in bending could depend on the ambient temperature. The absence of a waterproofing layer could increase the rate of deterioration significantly and this could be critical if the assessment model relied on transverse distribution and the bridge was transversely post-tensioned.

8.5.2 Limited remaining life

If it is known for certain that a structure is to be replaced in say 10–15 years then there is a good argument for allowing the full contribution of the doubtful factor. It is not easy to give hard and fast rules about this and each case must be considered on its merits and thoroughly examined before a decision is made.

8.5.3 Re-testing

There is the option of retesting the structure in the future to find out whether the questionable mechanism is still contributing at the same level to the strength of the structure. Such tests need not be as elaborate as the original test since it may only be necessary to obtain results for a few critical reference points. However, it is important that detailed records are kept of the original test, including weather and temperature conditions, so that the tests can be repeated as accurately as possible.

8.5.4 Monitoring of unreliable actions

Monitoring can be a means of confirming the continuing reliability of factors included in the assessment and can sometimes utilize unrecovered instrumentation from the load test. If this is not the case specific monitoring has to be set up for either measurement during regular site visits or increasingly, remotely, via an appropriate communications link. Again monitoring may only be required at a few critical reference points.

8.5.5 Types of hidden strength

Generally there will be more confidence placed upon those additional sources of strength where there is some physical feature of the structure which ensures that they are always mobilized. Thus there may be attachments to a steel beam which allow it to act compositely with the surrounding concrete even though the attachments may not be recognized shear connectors. The general response and overall behaviour of the structure during the load test could also be a source of confidence in predicting its long-term load-carrying capacity. A structure which behaves much as predicted, albeit with lower deformations and strains, is likely to inspire greater confidence than one whose behaviour is unexpected. In some cases it may be possible, by making relatively minor modifications to the structure, to ensure that the questionable mechanism continues to be effective in the longer term. For instance if compressive membrane action in the deck of a beam and slab bridge is to be relied upon it may be necessary to provide transverse straps to ensure that the edge beams do not move sideways under the effects of any transverse compressive forces in the slab.

8.6 Preparation of report

The test report should form a part of the comprehensive report on the complete assessment of the structure. The report should include the reasons for and the objectives of the test, a description of the test itself and the results obtained. The report should describe how the results have been used to modify the analytical process and the effect of these modifications on the assessment. Based on these findings the report should recommend what loads it is safe for the bridge to carry, detail any remedial actions that need to be taken, estimate the overall residual life of the bridge and whether further load testing or monitoring is required in the future.

The assumptions made in arriving at the safe load-carrying capacity should be clearly stated, especially those which may be subject to question. It is important that the reasoning behind any decision should be clearly stated.

9 References

Broomhead, S.F. and Clark, G.W. (1994). Strengthening masonry arches. *Proceedings of Bridge Modification Conference*, 1994, pp. 174–184. Thomas Telford, London.

Building Research Establishment (1995). *BRE Digest* 409. Masonry and concrete structures. Measuring in situ stress and elasticity using flat jacks.

Clark, G.W. (1995). Assessment of imperfect arches. *Proceedings of Structural Faults and Repair Conference* 1995, pp. 219–222. Institution of Civil Engineers, London.

Construction (Design and Management) Regulations (1994). HMSO. London. 1995.

Cullington, D.W. and Beales, C. (1995). Is your strengthening really necessary? *Proceedings of Bridge Modification Conference*, 1994, pp. 270–284. Thomas Telford, London.

Harvey W.J. (1995). Arch bridge testing. *Seminar on Analysis and Testing of Bridges*, April 1995. Institution of Structural Engineers, London.

Highways Agency (1998). *Design Manual for Roads and Bridges*. The Stationery Office, London.

Hughes, T.G. and Pritchard, R. (1997). In situ measurement of dead and live load stresses in a masonry arch. *Engineering Structures*, Vol. 19. Elsevier, London.

Mackay, D.C. (1995). Recent experiences on concrete and cast iron bridges. *Seminar on Analysis and Testing of Bridges*, April 1995. Institution of Structural Engineers, London.

Melbourne, C. (1990). The assessment of masonry arch bridges – the effects of defects. bridge management, inspection, maintenance and repair. *Proceedings of the First International Conference on Bridge Management*. Elsevier, London.

Packham, A.J. (1993). Cost effective load testing of bridges on British Railways. Bridge management, inspection, maintenance and repair. *Proceedings of the Second International Conference on Bridge Management*. Elsevier, London.

Page, J. (1994). Supplementary load testing and ultimate load testing: part 2: masonry arch bridges. Seminar on load testing for bridge assessment. *The Surveyor*. RILEM, London.

RILEM (1994). *RILEM Technical Recommendations for the Testing and Use of Construction Material*, pp. 503–508. E. & F.N. Spon, London.

Road Vehicles (Construction and Use) Regulations (1986). Statutory instrument 1986:1078 as amended by SIs 1986:1597; 1987:676 and 1133; 1988:271, 1178, 1287, 1524 and 1871.

Yeoell, D., Blakelock, R. and Munson S.R. (1993). The assessment, load testing and strengthening of Westminster Bridge. Bridge management, inspection, maintenance and repair. *Proceedings of the Second International Conference on Bridge Management*. Elsevier, London.

Appendix A: model specification of a supplementary load test

The following model specification provides the minimum requirements for carrying out a supplementary load test.

For highway structures the Technical Approval Authority is as defined in the *Design Manual for Roads and Bridges* (DMRB). For other bridge owners the TAA is defined as the Client.

A1 Supplementary load testing

A1.1 Supplementary load testing shall be considered to be part of the assessment process and shall only be undertaken after a full inspection, assessment and structural analysis has been carried out.

A1.2 Approval in principle (AIP) should be obtained from the appropriate Technical Approval Authority (TAA).

A2 Identification of requirements

A2.1 Prior to any load testing a pre-test analysis shall be carried out to identify the nature and location of any structural deficiencies and shortfalls in load capacity.

A2.2 The pre-test analysis shall identify any possible structural actions that have not been included in the assessment, but which could contribute to an increase in load capacity.

A2.3 The structural analysis should categorize any additional un-assessed structural actions according to evidence that they will remain effective at the ultimate limit state.

A2.4 The Engineer shall provide, for AIP by the TAA, a clear proposal that demonstrates how a load test will be able to evaluate and distinguish between any additional un-assessed structural actions. The proposal will give full details of the location and magnitude of applied test loads, the methods of application, the positions of instruments, the measurements to be taken and how these measurements are to be utilized to refine the assessment model.

A2.5 The proposal shall consider the need to carry out testing to confirm the magnitude of existing dead load stress in the structure.

A2.6 The Engineer shall provide the TAA with a list of any items of work in the proposal which, subject to approval of the TAA, are to be commissioned from other specialist consultants or contractors.

A2.7 The Engineer shall undertake a risk assessment based upon a proper consideration of the probability and consequences of failure occurring during the load testing of the structure.

A2.8 The Engineer shall inform the TAA of any proposed activities which may cause superficial damage to surfacing, waterproofing, surface coatings, concrete protection to reinforcement, or masonry. Any proposed activities which may cause superficial damage will only be carried out subject to the approval of the TAA.

A3 Planning the test

A3.1 The Engineer shall plan and carry out the test in compliance with the Construction (Design and Management) Regulations (1994).

A3.2 The Engineer shall visit the site to confirm that no significant increase in deterioration has taken place and access for testing and instrumentation is possible. A meeting with the police and relevant authorities should take place to ascertain what traffic management and other measures are required in order to carry out the test and ensure the safety of the public.

A3.3 The Engineer shall determine the number and location of any services laid within the bridge and provide additional protection to these services where required by the service authority.

A3.4 The Engineer shall provide the TAA with a programme for carrying out the load test detailing all activities and the estimated times for each together with any float time.

A3.5 The Engineer shall determine from the pre-test analysis the limits of loading, strain and deflection, at the critical points in the structure, beyond which the test will not be continued.

A4 Carrying out the test

A4.1 The Engineer will appoint one person to be test controller. The test controller will be a chartered engineer experienced in load testing and will have sole responsibility for directing the test, deciding the load levels within the planned limits and terminating the test should this become necessary.

A4.2 The test shall be stopped if any response reaches the planned limits determined from the pre-test analysis. When this occurs the relevant point in the structure shall be investigated, and the test only continued where the result is clearly in error and can be identified with a rectifiable failure in the measuring instrument.

A4.3 During the test the Engineer shall provide for an adequate means of communication between site staff and the test controller.

A4.4 All site staff shall be supplied with a copy of the test plan and be fully briefed on their tasks prior to the commencement of testing.

A4.5 Where data are to be logged electronically the Engineer shall provide facilities to back up data to an independent storage device both during and at the end of the test.

A4.6 The Engineer shall ensure that all electronic data logging equipment is connected to a stabilized non-interruptible power supply.

A4.7 Where requested the Engineer shall make available to the TAA, copies of all data collected during the test.

A4.8 On completion of the test the Engineer shall remove all equipment and vehicles, obscure any temporary road markings, make good any superficial damage to the structure and ensure the site is secure and safe to re-open to the public.

A5 Reporting

A5.1 In the first instance the Engineer shall produce a short factual summary report which details any unusual results or observations recorded during the test and confirms whether any urgent action is required.

A5.2 The final test report shall be produced as part of the complete assessment of the structure. It will include the objectives of the test, a description of the test and the results obtained. It will describe how the results were used to modify the analysis and the effect this has had on the assessment. It will make recommendations on the safe load-carrying capacity, detail any remedial actions necessary, estimate the overall residual life of the bridge and whether load testing will need to be repeated in the future.

Appendix B: measurement of existing stresses

B1   Introduction

When considering carrying out a load test on an existing structure it can be important to quantify the level of existing stress in the critical elements. Often this cannot be reliably assessed by calculation and in many cases there is some doubt that particular structural elements carry the level of load that calculations predict.

There are several methods available for measuring the residual stresses in both concrete and metal structures. These stresses may arise from the dead loads carried by the structure and from unforeseen support settlements which have taken place since the structure was built. In pre-stressed concrete structures there will also be the effects of the forces generated by the prestressing tendons. All the techniques use the principle of strain relief to determine stresses at a particular point in the structure. They rely on some removal of material, usually by hole/core drilling or slot cutting to obtain a release of strain. The measured strain release is then used to calculate the existing stresses at that point.

Skill is required for interpreting the results as they are total stresses and can include manufacturing stresses caused by surface shrinkage in concrete or the hot rolling of steel sections and plate. Manufacturing stresses typically cause a distortion of the strain profile with depth which can be difficult to interpret.

Residual stresses in structures, particularly those in continuous structures, can be very much influenced by the ambient temperature at the time of measurement. Hence it is important that, where residual stresses are measured, temperatures are also recorded. It is necessary not only to record the ambient temperature but also the temperature of the structure itself since there may well be a temperature gradient from the top surface to the bottom surface of the structure. Where measurements have to be repeated at a later date it is important that the weather conditions should be as similar as possible.

It should be noted that stress determination methods are specialized techniques and that, despite their apparent simplicity, they should be undertaken by experienced specialist consultants/contractors if they are to provide meaningful results. The techniques are also potentially damaging and should only be carried out after careful consideration of any likely effects on the structure. Currently these methods are either carried out in full by specialist consultants or by specialized measurement companies in association with experienced consultants who provide the structural analysis expertise.

B2 Steel plate, cast and wrought iron

The original centre hole technique was developed by Mathar (1934) for the determination of stresses in steel. Currently, the test uses a specific strain gauge array (062RE) which is designed to be used in conjunction with the drilling of a 1.6 mm hole. To carry out the technique the gauge array is fixed to the plate at the required location and the hole is drilled incrementally using a high-speed air turbine to a depth of 1.6 mm. From the strain release recorded it is possible to calculate principal stresses with depth down to 0.8 mm (half the depth of the hole) below the surface of the steel. The use of the high-speed drill is necessary to ensure that stresses are not induced in the material by the drilling process. This test can be difficult to use on structural steel plate because of locked-in stresses caused by hot rolling and fabrication processes. It has however, together with a larger version using a 3.2 mm hole, been used effectively on cast iron where the manufacturing stresses are in general limited to within 1 mm of the surface. It has also been found to be successful for use on wrought iron.

The problem with the determination of stresses in structural steel plate is that the stress variation due to the manufacturing process is generally through the full thickness of the plate and can be complex. Typically the manufacturing stresses in a hot rolled plate will be compressive on the surface, changing to a sub-surface tensile peak before becoming compressive again at the centre. This problem has been solved by increasing the size of the centre hole and fixing a strain gauge rosette composed of individual gauges around the location of the hole. Again the hole is not conventionally drilled so as to avoid unwanted stresses.

In general any hot-rolled steel section which has not been normalized will have manufacturing stresses related to the way in which it cooled after rolling. Rolled steel beams for example will cool from the tips of the flanges and also from the centre of the web, which is usually the thinnest part of the section. This results in stress profiles going from compression at the flange tips to tension at the centre with the opposite effect on the web. Any tests and analysis to determine in situ stresses on rolled steel sections must therefore take account of these effects.

The accuracy of this method for use on structural steel is quoted as $\pm 10 \text{ N/mm}^2$.

B3 Prestressing tendons

The original centre hole technique has been developed to enable it to be used for determining the stresses in prestressing wires and tendons. As the stresses in tendons are largely uniaxial a two strain gauge array is used with one gauge on each side of the hole location. The hole is 1.6 mm diameter and 1.0 mm deep and is drilled incrementally. The analysis is complicated by the fact that the wire is round, i.e. the drill does not produce a round hole until it reaches a point where the chord is greater than its diameter. The analysis is further complicated with strand due to the centre wire being straight and the outside wires being wound; the modulus of the strand is slightly less than the modulus of the wire. In general, due to the consistent manufacture of wire and strand the manufacturing stresses are fairly well known. However, repeat tests on an unstressed section of material could be carried out if confirmation was required.

B4 Concrete

In any reinforced or prestressed structure measurement of stresses in the reinforcement or tendons will only provide local stresses from which the global stresses have to be determined. Measurement of stresses in the concrete can give a more global view of what is happening at a particular section in the structure.

B5 Coring methods

The most widely used technique involves coring the structure incrementally to obtain a release of strain. Two similar techniques are in general use. One uses an array of eight VW gauges located radially around a core position. Demec points are fixed in the same axis as the VW gauges, such that strain measurements can be taken across the core hole and on the core itself. The core is drilled incrementally with strain measurements taken from the VW gauges and demec points at each increment. The removed core is tested to determine the elastic modulus of the concrete (Mehrkar-Asl, 1988).

After completion of the first stage of the test a special cylindrical jacking assembly can be placed in the hole and used to partially restore the released strain in each of the gauge directions in turn while the VW gauge readings are recorded. Analysis is then carried out to determine the strains longitudinally and perpendicular to the jack.

Principal stresses are calculated from the strain release on the three different measuring systems. The strain release on the core will be total but the release on the surrounding demec and VW gauges will depend on their location relative to the hole. The results therefore are subject to conversion factors obtained from laboratory tests. The accuracy is quoted conservatively at $\pm 1 \text{ N/mm}^2$ although $\pm 0.5 \text{ N/mm}^2$ has been achieved during laboratory calibration.

A second type of test, developed independently, uses an array of eight VW gauges designed to be read with a single detachable plucking coil. With this test the VW gauges are positioned closer to the core hole and demec gauges are not used. A single VW gauge is positioned on the core in the direction, where known, of the major principal stress. The core is drilled incrementally with strain readings taken at each increment. When the core is cut to half depth it is broken out and the bottom of the hole flattened with a special diamond face plate. The central VW gauge is then re-attached to the flattened surface and the remaining half of the core cut as before. The elastic modulus is determined by testing the recovered core sections and also by undertaking a jacking test in the hole (Owens, 1993).

The results from the test are analysed and calibrated based on laboratory testing and an accuracy of $\pm 0.5 \text{ N/mm}^2$ is quoted for compressive stresses greater than 2 N/mm^2.

B6 Small hole coring

A different method of stress determination has been developed by Owens *et al.* (1994) for areas where there is insufficient space to carry out a core test. The method relies on the strain relief between several small cores cut close to each other. The holes are spaced sufficiently to allow a VW gauge to be mounted between them and the pattern adopted depends on whether unidirectional or principal stresses are required. Cores are 35 or 40 mm diameter cut to a depth of 35 or 45 mm, respectively. Again the results are calibrated from laboratory tests.

B7 Slot cutting

There are two methods of determining in situ stress using incremental slot cutting for the strain release. The first simply uses the strain release measured on either side of the slot by two VW gauges together with the elastic modulus obtained from coring to calculate the in situ stress. This method is usually carried out in conjunction with conventional coring tests elsewhere in the deck to determine the lateral stress distribution.

The second slot cutting method utilizes pressure compensation to restore the strain field using a special type of flat jack, with the in situ stress being calculated from the applied pressure in the jack. The flat jacks are made to a series of different secant sizes to enable the correct size to be fitted to each increment of the slot as it is cut. The technique was first developed by Abdunur (1985) and has now been further refined. With this method two steel bars are mounted either side of the slot position with VW gauges fixed between them at each end. The gauges effectively span the slot but are clear of the saw and can remain in place whilst the saw is cutting. At each increment the correct size of flat jack is inserted in the slot and pressurized to restore the original strain condition.

As the original strain field is theoretically restored the elastic modulus of the concrete is not required and the test is also unaffected by the presence of reinforcement. A calibration has to be used however, to compensate for initial jack stiffness and creep during the test. The effects of cutting temperature have been largely eliminated by the cutting equipment now adopted. The method is claimed to be more accurate than coring tests at low stress but provides only uniaxial stresses.

The flat jack technique has been developed for the determination of stress in masonry structures. This has been tried before with limited success; however, a more flexible jack and improvements in strain measurement have been developed and proved successful in measuring in situ stresses in arches and masonry tunnel linings.

B8 References for Appendix B

Abdunur, C. (1985). Stress measurement in structures by a miniaturized stress release method. *Bulletin de Liaison des Laboratiores des Ponts et Chaussees*, No. 138, July–August.

Owens, A. (1993). In-situ stress determination used in structural assessment of concrete structures. *Strain*, November, pp. 115–123.

Owens, A., Begg, D.W., Gratton, D.N, and Devane, M.A. (1994). A new in situ stress determination technique for concrete bridges. Bridge assessment, management and design. *Proceedings of the Centenary Year Bridge Conference*, 1994. Cardiff.

Mathar, J. (1934). Determination of initial stresses by measuring the deformation around drilled holes. *Trans ASME* **56**, 249–254.

Mehrker-Asl, S. (1988). Direct measurement of stress in concrete structures. PhD thesis, University of Surrey.

Appendix C: risk analysis

The following risk analysis procedure has been developed and is discussed in detail in Section 4.6.

Risk analysis of damage resulting from bridge load tests

Table C1   Factors influencing the probability of total/partial collapse or weakening

Factors		Criteria		Weighting	Max score	Min score
The quantity and quality of documented information (as-built drawings/calculations assessments)	3 None	2 Some relevant data	1 Full as-built records	2	6	2
Proneness of structure to brittle type failure (see C1 for suggested criteria scores)	3 Likely	3 Not known	1 Unlikely	3	9	3
Proneness of element to brittle/buckling type failure (see C2 for suggested criteria scores)	3 Likely	3 Not known	1 Unlikely	2	6	2
Condition of critical elements (deck beams/slabs)	3 Poor	2 Fair	1 Good	2	6	2
Condition of other elements (bearings, piers)	3 Poor	2 Fair	1 Good	1	3	1
Possible hidden significant defects	3 Likely	3 Not known	1 Unlikely	2	6	2
Performance of structure under current traffic	3 Poor	2 Fair	1 Good	3	9	3
			Totals	45	15

All of the above factors influence the probability of each of the events considered (total collapse, partial collapse, weakening).

Below are some suggested criteria scores for structural materials, details and elements.

C1 Scores for structures (taken as a whole)

C1.1 Materials of main construction

C1.1.1 Metal	Cast iron	3
	Wrought iron	2
	Steel	1

| C1.1.2 Concrete | Over reinforced | 3 |
| | Under reinforced | 1 |

Prestressed	Post-tensioned segmental	3
	Post-tensioned in situ	3
	Post-tensioned precast	1

C1.2 Features of main construction

C1.2.1 Multi-span with tie downs

| Tie downs not inspectable | 3 |
| Tie downs inspectable | 1 |

| C1.2.2 Longitudinal beams with masonry jack arches | 2 |

C2 Scores for load-bearing elements of structure

C2.1 Scores for load-bearing elements of structure

C2.1.1 Compression flanges		
	Unrestrained flanges	3
	Flanges restrained by friction	2
	Fully restrained flanges	1

| C2.1.2 Columns/compression struts | Slender columns/struts | 3 |
| | Short columns/struts | 1 |

| C2.1.3 Stiffeners | Bearing stiffeners | 3 |
| | Intermediate stiffeners | 2 |

| C2.1.4 Steel web panels | Unstiffened | 3 |
| | Stiffened | 2 |

A typical example showing the calculation of the probability score is shown below.

Consider a bridge which meets the following criteria for the factors in Table C1:

	Criteria score	Weighting factor	Combined score
• has drawings but no calculations available	2	2	4
• brittle failure of structure unlikely	1	3	3
• brittle/buckling failure of component unlikely	1	2	2
• critical elements in moderate condition	2	2	4
• other elements in good condition	1	1	1
• hidden defects are likely	3	2	6
• has fair performance under traffic	2	3	6
	Total		26

Thus 26 is a measure of the probability of one of the above events occurring. Because of the way in which the scoring is structured, a relatively high total score will indicate a greater probability of collapse whereas a relatively low total score would indicate that some weakening of the structure is the more likely event.

Note that the maximum score possible is 45 and the minimum is 15. The total score can be normalized on a scale of 1–10 as follows:

$$\left\{ \left\{ \left[\frac{score - min}{max - min} \right] \times 9 \right\} + 1 \right. \tag{C1}$$

In this example the normalized score would be $((26 - 15) \div (45 - 15) \times 9) + 1 = 4.3$.

Since some consequences do not relate to all events the total possible consequence score will differ for each event as shown here.

Event	Maximum consequence score	Minimum consequence score
Total or partial collapse	339	113
Weakening	39	13

Note that zero criteria scores may be used for certain consequences in particular situations, for example:

if the bridge carries no services
if there is no risk of death/serious injury
if diversion is not necessary

$\left.\right\}$ If zero criteria scores are used the normalized minimum may become less than 1.

Example of calculation of consequence score

Consider the event of partial collapse at a particular bridge:

Consequence	Criteria score	Weighting factor	Combined consequence score
Serious injury (on or under bridge)	0	100	0
Importance of railway in route network	2	2	4
Importance of road in route network	2	2	4
Divert traffic	2	2	4
Duration	1	2	2
Strengthen	1	3	3
Disruption to services in bridge	0	2	0
		Total	17

As before the score can be normalized on a scale of 1–10 by substituting into formula (C1) above. For this example the normalized score would be $((17 - 11) \div (33 - 11) \times 9) + 1 = 3.5$.

This is a measure of the consequences of partial collapse. A score near 1 would indicate relatively minor consequences whereas a score approaching 10 would indicate very serious consequences (see Figure C1).

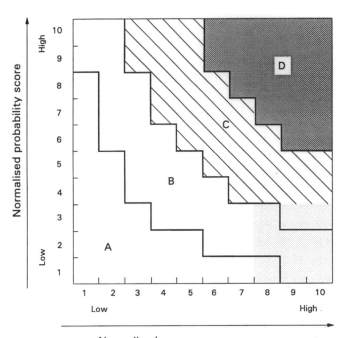

Normalised consequences score

Combinations that identify situations of the highest concern and load testing should not be undertaken

Combinations that identify situations of considerable concern and should only be load tested by Category C specialists defined below

Combinations that may require inspection for credible events

A   Bridges that fall into this category can be tested by experienced Engineers/Consultants with due regard to the provisions of this document

B   Bridges that fall into this category should be tested by Specialist Consultants experienced in bridge load testing

C   Bridges that fall into this category should only be tested by Specialist Consultants with considerable structural knowledge and testing experience of this particular type of structure

Figure C1   Qualitative risk-based ranking matrix.

D   Do not load test

Risk of an event occurring

Risk represents a combination of the probability of an event occurring and the potential consequences if it does occur

$$\text{risk} = \text{probability} \times \text{consequences}$$

Thus, we can get a measure of risk by multiplying our normalized total probability and total consequence scores. This would give a normalized range for risk of approximately 1–100.

In our example the normalized risk score would be $4.3 \times 3.5 = 15$.

Based on the normalized risk range the following criteria have been set:

1. To avoid undue risk of a partial collapse do not carry out a load test if the normalized risk score is greater than or equal to 50. In other words there is a high risk of partial collapse if the normalized risk score (NRS) >50.
2. There is a significant risk of partial collapse if (NRS) >25 and tests should only be carried out by consultants with specialist knowledge of the particular type of structure.
3. There is a lower risk of partial collapse if (NRS) <25.

Clearly there is a subjective element in choosing the (NRS) criteria.

Note

There is a considerable subjective element in selecting the probability and consequence weighting factors used earlier. The selection of the probability and consequence criteria scores should be reasonably objective if sensible criteria are used.

Summary of risk analysis process

1. Consider the events whose risk of occurrence you want to assess, for example, the risk that a load test will cause total collapse of the bridge.
2. Look for data types that will help you to assess the probability of occurrence.
3. For each of these data types set and rank criteria that different bridges could meet.
4. For each of these data types decide on a weighting factor based on the relative usefulness of the data for deciding the probability of the event occurring.
5. Work out the probability score and normalize it.

In this case the criteria are ranked 1–3 but the scores have been normalized on a scale of 1–10.

If some criteria are ranked 0–3 the normalized range will be a number less than 1, for example, 0.8–10.

6. Look for consequences that may arise if the event occurs.
7. For each consequence set and rank criteria that load tests on different bridges could meet.
8. For each consequence decide on a weighting factor based on the relative importance of the consequence.
9. Work out the consequence score and normalize it.
10. Determine the normalized risk score (NRS) by calculating the product of the normalized probability and consequence scores. The range of the NRS is obtained from the products of the normalized maxima and minima of the possible probability and consequence scores.
11. Set risk criteria for the event (high, medium, low) based on the NRS in particular cases.

Appendix D: case studies

Case study 1

D1 Description of bridge

The bridge was built in the mid-1950s with a clear span of 10.05 m and carries an unclassified road over a river. The deck consists of pre-cambered precast post-tensioned concrete beams (450 mm wide × 305 mm deep) with mortar packing in between. The larger parapet beams on each edge are separated from the main deck by service bays. Both longitudinal and transverse prestressing use cables composed of 5 mm wires. The six discrete transverse cables pass through small precast strut beams joining the parapet beams across the service bays to the main deck. There is no topping slab and surfacing is laid directly on the beams. The cross-section is illustrated in Figure D1.

D2 Outline of problem

The bridge was to be assessed for its load-carrying capacity as part of the bridge assessment programme. Because of the absence of a topping slab and a waterproofing membrane there were questions over the effectiveness of the transverse prestressing cables which could have been corroded by leakage through the deck. As the transverse load distribution of the deck was fundamental to its load-carrying capacity any loss of transverse prestress due to corroded wires could have had serious implications for the assessed capacity of the bridge. Rather than make conservative assumptions about the effectiveness of the transverse prestress it was decided to measure the actual load distribution characteristics by means of a load test.

D3 Objectives of load test

The main objective of the load test was to determine the transverse distribution characteristics of the bridge deck under live loads. The effectiveness of the distribution was to be determined from the percentage of the overall live load-bending moment carried by the individual beams. In addition a check was to be made as to whether there were any restraints at the abutments which might have affected the structural behaviour.

D4 Arrangements for load test

D4.1 Loading

The loading was applied at mid-span from the rear axles of a single lorry and then two lorries side by side. The intensity of the loading, 5 tonnes per axle, was chosen in the light of knowledge, obtained from in situ stress measurements, about the extent of pre-stress loss in the longitudinal and transverse cables (see Section D5). The load intensity had to be sufficient to give a measurable strain without causing permanent damage to the bridge. The transverse positions of the axles are shown in Figure D2.

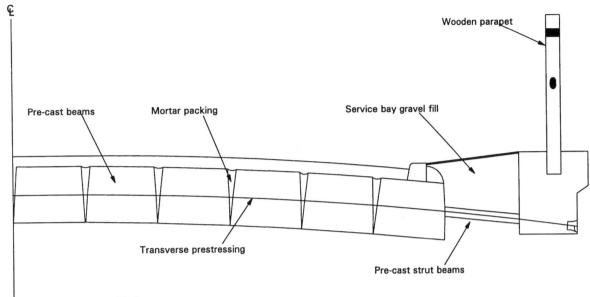

Figure D1   Cross-section of deck.

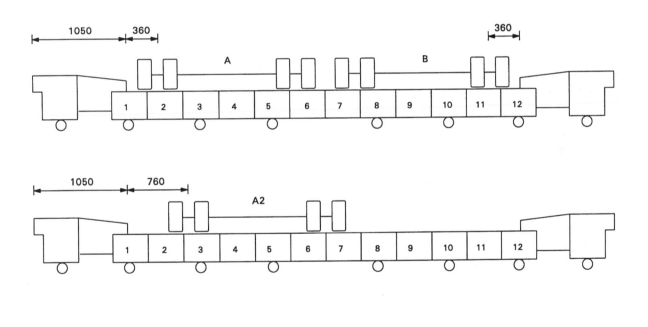

○ **VW gauge positions**

Figure D2   Transverse position of axles.

D4.2   Instrumentation   The deck was instrumented at mid-span with vibrating wire gauges fixed both in the longitudinal and transverse directions on the beam soffits and across the joints as shown in Figure D3. In addition two beams were instrumented with VW gauges along their length to detect whether any restraints existed at the abutments which might have affected the behaviour of the deck.

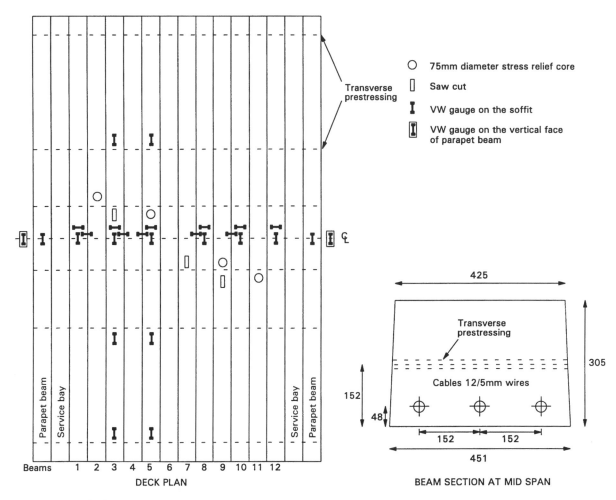

Figure D3   Details of instrumentation.

D5   Other measurements

The remaining levels of pre-stress in both the longitudinal and transverse directions were assessed from residual stress measurements taken from four stress relief cores and four saw cuts. The positions of the test points which were chosen to provide a representative sample of the stresses in the deck are shown in Figure D3. The results showed a 47% loss of prestress in the longitudinal direction and a complete loss of prestress in the transverse direction.

D6   Analysis of results

The longitudinal strains measured during the load test were used to estimate the total induced moment in the deck which was compared with the theoretical applied live load moment. The results compared very favourably with an uncracked section with an E-value identical to the measured value. Figure D4 illustrates the measured relative percentages of bending moment carried by the monitored beams, compared with the theoretical value if the beam in question carried the whole weight of one side of the lorry with no transverse distribution.

The pattern of measured strains (subsequently translated into bending moments) is consistent with what would be expected from a deck that had reasonably good transverse distribution characteristics, as shown by the symmetry obtained from the two-

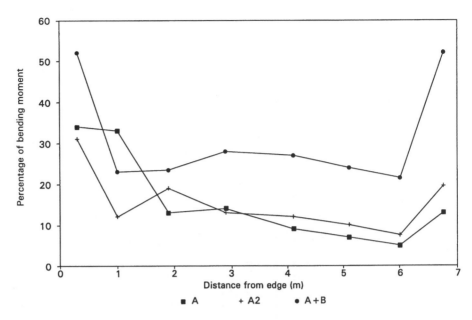

Figure D4   Percentage of bending moment per beam.

lorry loading case (A + B) in Figure D4. A somewhat surprising result from this was the strong transverse distribution to the outer parapet beams through what appears to be rather flexible discrete transverse connections.

The transverse strains across the joints were very variable and changed markedly with changes in the load pattern. The transverse strains in the beam soffits themselves were very small and did not follow the same pattern as those across the joints, thus confirming the lack of continuity across the joints.

D7   Use of results

The results from the load test provided evidence of a much greater transverse distribution of loading at the critical mid-span section than could have safely been assumed taking into account the probable corrosion of the transverse prestressing. This in turn led to a significant improvement in the assessed load-carrying capacity of the structure which was obtained by feeding the information into the elastic computer analysis. Although it was recognized that load distribution characteristics can change as the level of loading increases it was considered that it was acceptable to use the load characteristics of the deck under test loads in conjunction with the ultimate loading criteria to determine the capacity of the bridge at the ultimate limit state.

The extrapolation up to the theoretical ultimate condition was partly justified by the fact that it would be impossible to attain the full intensity of HA loading to BD37/88 by filling the plan area of the deck with laden lorries. Also it was noted that the longitudinal prestressing appeared to be in good condition so that any failure of the transverse distribution mechanism was unlikely to lead to a catastrophic collapse.

Case study 2

D8   Description of bridge

The bridge was built in 1850 with a clear span of approximately 9.3 m and carries a trunk road over a canal. The deck has an arch profile and is constructed from 12 cast-iron cambered I-beams with buckled plates supported between the lower flanges. The buckled plates and the ends of the beams are covered by a concrete overlay. The road profile is made up from fill material with an asphalt topping (see Figures D5 and D6).

Figure D5   General elevation of the bridge.

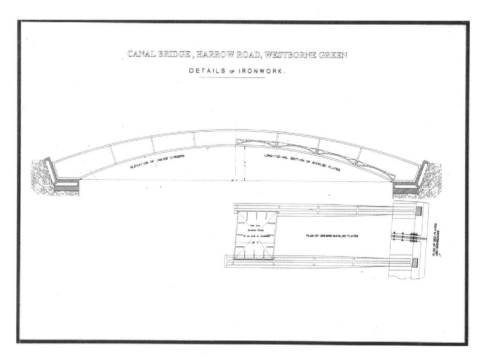

CANAL BRIDGE, HARROW ROAD, WESTBORNE GREEN

DETAILS OF IRONWORK.

Figure D6

D9   Outline of problem

The bridge deck was assessed as part of the bridge assessment programme but failed to meet the current assessment criteria when analysed by conventional methods. Due to the lack of shear studs or other connections it was assumed that there was no interaction between the girders and the infill concrete. On the basis of this assessment, a 7.5-tonne gross vehicle weight limit would have been necessary. However, without supportive information on the behaviour of the structure, the necessarily simplistic analysis was extremely conservative and based on the longitudinal cast iron beam sections alone. The importance of the route on which this bridge lies is such that any restriction would be unacceptable.

recognized that this would be conservative since membrane effects and partial restraint at the supports could not be modelled and the beneficial effects of the surfacing would be ignored. It was recommended that a further analysis should be performed if the load rating obtained from the improved grillage analysis was still below acceptable levels, as additional capacity was likely to be achieved by carrying out a more sophisticated thin shell membrane analysis of the deck.

Case study 3

D15 Description of bridge

The bridge comprises 22 steel and cast-iron girders and concrete infill to form an infill joist slab-type deck with a span of approximately 7 m. The deck is supported on brick abutments with concrete pad stones beneath the girders. The cast-iron girders were part of the original structure which was modified in approximately 1905, these girders being retained in the footway construction (see Figures D9 and D10).

D16 Outline of problem

The bridge deck was assessed as part of the bridge assessment programme but failed to meet the current assessment criteria when analysed by conventional methods. The assessment was carried out using simple methods of load distribution for the longitudinal members and took no account of the potential interaction between the girders and the infill concrete. However, without supportive information on the behaviour of the structure, the necessarily simplistic analysis was extremely conservative and based on the longitudinal beam sections alone.

D17 Objectives of load test

Load tests were carried out on the deck to determine the transverse distribution characteristics and the existence of any composite action under the loads used. The tests were also devised to determine any encastre effects at the abutments which would lead to further reductions in the mid-span stresses under live loading. Separate tests were carried out on the carriageway and footway to determine the proportion of load transmitted between these two parts of the structure. The degree of transverse

Figure D9   General elevation of the bridge

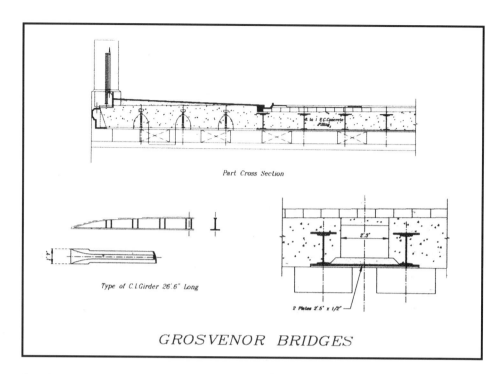

GROSVENOR BRIDGES

Figure D10

distribution and the effective stiffness of the section were determined from the live load bending moments induced in the individual beams. Any fixity at the abutments was assessed using the strain profiles induced along selected beams under both dead and live load.

D18
Arrangements for load test

D18.1 Loading

The deck was tested initially using three 17.5-tonne lorries positioned on the carriageway and then with two 7.5-tonne lorries on the footway. During the first loading stage, the larger lorries were driven on the carriageway one at a time and positioned abreast in the westbound inside lane, the westbound outside lane and the eastbound outside lane in turn.

The second stage involved loading the north footway. The loads were applied by driving one of the lorries on the footpath and positioning the back axle at mid-span. A second vehicle was driven on the footpath behind the first lorry and positioned as close as possible. Strain readings were taken as each of the lorries was positioned on the footway and as they were removed.

D18.2 Instrumentation

The deck was instrumented with 22 No. VW gauges attached to the soffit of a number of the beams. Longitudinal strains in 15 selected girders, across the width of the deck, were monitored at mid-span during the load tests to allow the transverse distribution to be determined. Additional gauges were positioned adjacent to the supports and quarter points of selected beams in the carriageway and footways to establish the presence of any encastre behaviour.

D19 Analysis of results

The tests carried out on this bridge demonstrated that the structure was behaving in a considerably superior manner to that predicted using either the steel or cast-iron beam sections alone or composite behaviour with no transverse distribution of load. The results confirmed that composite action existed between the beams and concrete infill and good transverse load distribution occurred within the bridge deck. In addition, the induced strains indicated that there was a significant degree of fixity at the supports. The tensile stresses in both the steel and the cast iron sections were considerably lower than anticipated. The maximum tensile stress in the steel sections was a tenth of that under the full carriageway test load assuming that the steel beam sections act alone with no transverse distribution of load. In the footways the tensile stresses were only a fifth of those assessed to be induced in the cast iron sections.

The membrane action present in the deck had not been allowed for in the initial analyses but was taken into account in the subsequent calculations. The behaviour of the deck under the applied loading and passing traffic loads suggested that the in-plane stiffness contributed significantly to its structural performance. The effective behaviour of the beams under the applied loads was shown to be as a composite section, with transverse distribution of a single axle at mid-span spread over a minimum of seven carriageway beams. It was also demonstrated that there was very little transverse distribution of carriageway live loading into the cast iron beams in the footway section.

D20 Use of results The results of the testing were used to modify the assessment of the structure using a non-linear analysis of the deck. A specialized program was used which allowed for membrane effects and the stiffness contribution from partially cracked concrete. It was considered that both of these effects were likely to be present in the deck and would lead to substantially better distribution properties and flexural stiffness. Although the analysis could not be modified sufficiently to fully model the effects observed on site, a conservative approach was sufficient to show the structure to be adequate to carry full assessment live loading.